Ben Goldstein's
30 Ideas
on Inclusion in ELT

Cambridge Handbooks for Language Teachers

Part of the award-winning Cambridge Handbooks for Language Teachers series, the Pocket Editions come in a handy, pocket-sized format and are crammed full of tips and ideas from experienced English language teaching professionals, to enrich your teaching practice.

Recent Pocket Editions:

Penny Ur's 100 Teaching Tips
PENNY UR

Jack C. Richards' 50 Tips for Teacher Development
JACK C. RICHARDS

Scott Thornbury's 30 Language Teaching Methods
SCOTT THORNBURY

Alan Maley's 50 Creative Activities
ALAN MALEY

Scott Thornbury's 101 Grammar Questions
SCOTT THORNBURY

Mark Hancock's 50 Tips for Teaching Pronunciation
MARK HANCOCK

Carol Read's 101 Tips for Teaching Primary Children
CAROL READ

David Crystal's 50 Questions About English Usage
DAVID CRYSTAL

Herbert Puchta's 101 Tips for Teaching Teenagers
HERBERT PUCHTA

Nicky Hockly's 50 Essentials of Using Learning Technologies
NICKY HOCKLY

Penny Ur's 77 Tips for Teaching Vocabulary
PENNY UR

Jeremy Harmer's 50 Communicative Activites
JEREMY HARMER

Philip Kerr's 30 Trends in ELT
PHILIP KERR

Sarah Mercer and Herbert Puchta's 101 Psychological Tips
SARAH MERCER AND HERBERT PUCHTA

Nicky Hockly's 30 Essentials for Using Artificial Intelligence
NICKY HOCKLY

Scott Thornbury's 66 Essentials of Lesson Design
SCOTT THORNBURY

Ben Goldstein's 30 Ideas on Inclusion in ELT

Ben Goldstein

Consultant and editor: Scott Thornbury

Shaftesbury Road, Cambridge CB2 8EA, United Kingdom

One Liberty Plaza, 20th Floor, New York, NY 10006, USA

477 Williamstown Road, Port Melbourne, VIC 3207, Australia

314–321, 3rd Floor, Plot 3, Splendor Forum, Jasola District Centre, New Delhi – 110025, India

103 Penang Road, #05–06/07, Visioncrest Commercial, Singapore 238467

Cambridge University Press & Assessment is a department of the University of Cambridge.

We share the University's mission to contribute to society through the pursuit of education, learning and research at the highest international levels of excellence.

www.cambridge.org
Information on this title: www.cambridge.org/9781009805742

© Cambridge University Press & Assessment 2025

First published 2025

20 19 18 17 16 15 14 13 12 11 10 9 8 7 6 5 4 3 2 1

Printed in Great Britain by CPI Group (UK) Ltd, Croydon CR0 4YY

A catalogue record for this publication is available from the British Library

ISBN 978-1-009-80574-2 Paperback
ISBN 978-1-009-80572-8 Cambridge Core

Contents

Acknowledgements and thanks

The authors and publishers acknowledge the following sources of copyright material and are grateful for the permissions granted. While every effort has been made, it has not always been possible to identify the sources of all the material used, or to trace all copyright holders. If any omissions are brought to our notice, we will be happy to include the appropriate acknowledgments on reprinting and in the next update to the digital edition, as applicable.

Key: PRE = Prelims, U = Unit.

Text

PRE: UNESCO for the adapted text from *A Guide for ensuring inclusion and equity in education* by UNESCO, 2017. Copyright © 2017 United Nations. Reproduced with kind permission; **U3:** Juan Lopes for the adapted text from Personal Correspondence (video) by Juan Lopes. Copyright © Juan Lopes. Reproduced with kind permission; Linguahouse for the adapted text from Thanksgiving by Stephanie Hirschman, 09.21.2023. Copyright © 2023 Linguahouse. Reproduced with kind permission; **U4:** Ready to Run video by DLA for the adapted text from Mainstreaming marginalized voices by Ben Goldstein, 11.11.2021. Copyright © 2021 Ready to Run video by DLA. Reproduced with kind permission.

Photography

Back cover: Ben Goldstein presenting to teachers at the Universidad de las Américas in Quito, Ecuador in 2025. Copyright © Epica Comunicación.

Typesetting

QBS Learning.

Thanks

A big thank you to Karen Momber and Jo Timerick for their enthusiasm and interest in this project in its early stages and to Simon Williamson subsequently. Many thanks also to Scott Thornbury for his great support and helpful suggestions during the writing and Alison Sharpe for her faultless editorial work. I also would like to thank Amanda Hawthorne for her ideas and feedback on the content. And a final thank you to my husband Daniel Isern for pushing me on and motivating me to write this book. I couldn't have done it without him.

Why I wrote this book

All learners are unique and diversity in the classroom has long been valued in language teaching. However, only recently has inclusion come to the forefront of our profession as it has done in many other walks of life. Consider, for example, how the representation of marginalized groups has evolved in mainstream media and marketing in recent years or how, on official forms, it is now common in some cultures to find a **non-binary** option tick box in the **gender** category. Likewise, consider how many companies now possess official 'inclusion statements' on their websites, EDI (equity, diversity and inclusion) departments to ensure employees do not face **discrimination** and request that their employees include their choice of pronouns in message signatures.

However, despite (or perhaps because of) this interest, negative attitudes towards inclusive practices have emerged at the same time. We live, after all, in an increasingly polarized world in which many of those in power actively, and at times violently, oppose an inclusive agenda. I believe this quotation by Nobel Prize winning author Toni Morrison sums up the attitude of many when confronted by difference or 'the other':

Why should we want to know the stranger
When it is easier to estrange one another?
Why should we want to close the distance
When we can close the gate?

It is urgent therefore that 'closing the distance' and 'knowing the stranger' – as Morrison puts it – become an intrinsic part of what we do as language teachers. Indeed, there are ethical, moral and political reasons for embracing inclusive practices in our work, not just pedagogical ones (see **5**).

And, depending on where you work, there may well be legal reasons to do so, too. Since 2017 when UNESCO published 'A Guide for Ensuring Inclusion and Equity in Education', many teachers have been expected to embrace inclusive practices in their programmes and curricula. Indeed, inclusive and equitable education is embedded in the UN's Sustainable Development Goals and viewed by many as lying at the very heart of a transformative education agenda.

As Ainscow (2020) has said referring to mainstream school education, inclusive practice can be justified not just on educational grounds but also socially and economically: socially, because inclusive schools are able to change attitudes to difference by educating all children together, and form the basis for a just and non-discriminatory society; and economically, as it is less costly to establish and maintain schools which educate all children together than set up specialist institutions.

However, while most language teachers appreciate the importance of adopting inclusive practices in their work, they lack the practical experience and know-how to do so effectively. There is a belief that employing such strategies will just add to their already heavy workload or that it will demand specialist knowledge. This is not helped by the fact that the terms we use to describe inclusive teaching practices vary from place to place. Indeed, the term *inclusion*, previously only associated with **disability** in educational contexts, nowadays extends to wider groups as a response to our increasingly diverse societies (see **1**).

Another more fundamental problem is the difficulty in creating inclusive classrooms in the first place. There may be resistance from students, teachers, school management, parents and even the community as a whole – all of whom may have strongly-held views on the subject. It is for this reason, as Sowton (2021, p. 21) says, 'that inclusive policies are most effective when supported by all the institution's educational stakeholders.' We all need to be involved in this enterprise and openness and collaboration are essential (see **F**).

It is for all the above reasons that I decided to write this book. Though the topic is of critical importance, handling it can be challenging and highly sensitive on a number of levels and teachers require guidance and support in order to do so successfully. Essentially, the aim of this handbook is to make that process a whole lot easier without trivializing it or becoming tokenistic.

Multiple Perspectives

My interest in inclusion emerged when I started my career as an ELT materials writer at the start of the 2000s. I realized, as so many others, that materials did not represent the world as I believed it should be represented and I felt that something had to be done. Content back then, as Kerr (2023, p. 23) has said, was often 'white-anglocentric, male dominated, and heteronormative' in nature and reflected 'culturally limited, middle-class values … often alien to the students for whom the material was intended'. Three decades later, although much has improved, the battle goes on precisely because certain marginalized groups are still excluded by publishers who wish their materials to appeal to the widest markets possible.

However, the topic of inclusion is much broader than this and materials represent just one section in this book (see **D**). You'll also find sections on key concepts, classroom strategies and activities, the classroom environment, assessment and working together. Throughout, you'll see that an all-encompassing and *holistic approach* to the topic has been adopted (see **1**).

Likewise, learner diversity is considered from *multiple perspectives*: gender, sexual orientation, age, social class, ethnic, cultural and religious identity as well as neurodivergence and physical disability. However, this is not the only way to categorize diversity, and it is worth bearing in mind that many learners may a) suffer from multiple forms of discrimination due to these differences (see **1**) and/or b) reject a particular label or a diagnosis which emphasizes this difference (see **3**).

In the ELT world, some worthwhile titles, both academic and practical, have been published on the subject of teaching students with **special educational needs (SEN)** – a term now gradually being phased out (see **3**) – but few have addressed inclusion *holistically*, taking into account the multiple perspectives described above. This book is therefore an attempt to address these perspectives in order to provide an accessible and practical guide to ensuring inclusion in *any* language classroom, both in physical and virtual spaces and for any age groups.

Importantly, due to its reduced format, the book does *not* aim to provide specific knowledge of learner diversity, and the ideas are not intended to be limited to one difference or another. For that reason, you won't find in-depth coverage of strategies on, for example, teaching dyslexic students or **refugees**. The idea here is to raise awareness of the diversity that you may encounter in class and highlight the areas that you need to consider in order to ensure *all* learners feel that they belong and can fulfill their potential. However, if there is a particular aspect of diversity that you want to look at in more detail, references and suggestions for further reading are provided, as are a glossary and an analysis of the terminology currently used in the profession. Glossary items are indicated in bold throughout the text. These cover as many areas of diversity as space allows (see also **3, 6**).

How to use this book

There are a couple of ways that you can read this book: either from cover to cover or by dipping into specific sections of interest as and when you need them. However, if you are unfamiliar with the basic concepts, then it would make sense to start with section A which unpacks the notion of inclusion and highlights the multiple benefits of adopting an inclusive approach.

I have labelled the thirty sections as 'ideas' because they represent, in reality, different considerations which can encompass concepts, strategies, activities and approaches, none of which should be considered prescriptive. The important thing to remember about them is that they belong to a broader procedure. Although many of the ideas here are easy to adopt, they will not make you an inclusive teacher overnight. Rather they should form part of an evolving process in your professional development. That is, in fact, the best way to understand the concept of inclusive practices as a '*process* that helps overcome the barriers which limit the presence, participation and achievement of learners' (UNESCO, 2017, p. 7). The book's structure also reflects this shift towards thinking of inclusive practice not simply as providing access and **accommodations**, but as removing obstacles which may undermine a student's ability to succeed. This is a key concern as we have all experienced barriers to learning at some point in our lives and, for that reason, it is hoped you will relate to many of the examples and contexts laid out here (see **2**).

Some of the tips and strategies may echo or expand upon activities and ideas which you are familiar with. That is because communicative language classrooms are, in themselves, good spaces for adopting inclusive practices as they should be both interactive and learner-centred. For example, opportunities for getting to know your learners and developing a good relationship with them are available from day one in the language classroom, as is, for example, promoting positive interaction and empathy (see **9**, **14**). What's more, many language materials aim to encourage intercultural competence which, in itself, requires an awareness of and respect for differences between and within cultures.

Finally, it is important to remember that an inclusive approach, though it may highlight students at risk of marginalization, exclusion or underachievement, should benefit *all* students not just those who are marginalized. From such a perspective, individual difference is seen as a source of diversity that is able to enhance the lives and learning of others. For example, strategies intended to work for neurodivergent students such as offering multi-sensory stimuli, reviewing language frequently, breaking content down into manageable chunks and so on, can and should work equally well for everybody in class.

So, whether these ideas build on your existing skills or knowledge or are entirely new for you, I hope that they will start you on the path of embracing inclusive teaching practices. Fundamentally, such practices engage students in learning which is meaningful, relevant and accessible, providing every learner with the chance to belong, to work together and to succeed in language learning.

Ainscow, M. (2020) Promoting inclusion and equity in education: lessons from international experiences. *Nordic Journal of Studies in Educational Policy*, 6(1), 7–16. https://doi.org/10.1080/20020317.2020.1729587

Kerr, P. (2023) *30 Trends in ELT*, Cambridge: Cambridge University Press & Assessment

Morrison, T. (2017) *The Origin of Others*, Harvard: Harvard University Press

Sowton, C. (2021) *Teaching in challenging circumstances,* Cambridge: Cambridge University Press & Assessment

UNESCO (2017) *A guide for ensuring inclusion and equity in education.* https://unesdoc.unesco.org/ark:/48223/pf0000248254, https://doi.org/10.54675/MHHZ2237

United Nations, 17 Sustainable Development Goals. https://sdgs.un.org/goals

A: Understanding inclusion

The topic of inclusion is a complex one, partly because it means different things to different people in different contexts. This initial section attempts to unpack the concepts that are necessary for understanding the topic at a broad level, including, crucially, the language used.

Key concepts

Inclusion is a complex term to define and has become politically loaded. It also involves us discussing a number of key interrelated concepts. These are therefore best defined from the start.

I have chosen *inclusion* both as an umbrella term and the title of this book, but you may well have heard other terms used in association with inclusion – in particular, the acronym EDI (standing for equality/equity, diversity and inclusion).

Other acronyms frequently used are EDIB (equality/equity, diversity, inclusion and belonging) or JEDI (justice, equality/equity, diversity and inclusion). This is revealing because inclusive practice is necessarily bound up with issues of belonging and justice. Indeed, living as we do at a time where there is increasing polarization in society and suspicion of 'the other', ideas surrounding inclusion are evolving to bring to the fore notions of social justice and intersectionality. For a more critical anlaysis of the term *inclusion* see **30**.

Diversity

Different characteristics that occur among individuals, including but not limited to, are: ability, age, body shape, cultural affiliation, **disability**, **ethnicity**, gender, gender identity, sexual orientation, language, migration, political affiliation, religious affiliation, national origin, **neurodiversity** and socio-economic status.

Equality/Equity

The terms are used interchangeably in some contexts (a quick Google search revealed that the 'E' in EDI and DEI stands for 'equality' and 'equity' in pretty much equal measure) but they refer to quite different things.

Equality means that everybody gets the same treatment, while *equity* refers to everybody getting what they need. Clearly, we do not all start out from the same place nor have the same needs, so if you apply the same criteria and treat all students equally, inevitably some will still do better than others.

The difference is, in reality, to do with results and actions. According to the UNESCO report 'All means All' (UNESCO, 2020, p. 11): 'Equality is a state of affairs (what): a result that can be observed in inputs, outputs or outcomes, e.g. achieving gender equality. Equity is a process (how): [these are the] actions aimed at ensuring equality.' In reality, striving for equity is about recognizing barriers and constraints and doing something to redress them. As Malone (2022, p. 87) says, 'the principle of equity acknowledges that there are historically undeserved and underrepresented populations and that fairness regarding these unbalanced conditions is needed to assist equality in the provision of effective opportunities to all groups.'

Inclusion

For me, inclusion is about creating an environment in which all students can be valued, respected and have equal access to opportunities and resources. It should be seen as a *process* involving practices that embrace diversity and build a sense of belonging and community in which all forms of discrimination are eliminated. In this respect I follow the OECD's (2023, pp. 27–28) line here: 'More than a particular policy or practice related to a specific group of students or individuals, this definition identifies an ethos of inclusion and communities of learners, which does not only involve an individual dimension but also a communal one' (see **30**).

It is important that inclusion is seen as a right of all citizens and should thus benefit everyone, not only those who might otherwise be excluded or marginalized. In the educational context, this means shifting the focus of inclusive practice from referring to those students with 'special needs' to a more *holistic* perspective which focuses on the *barriers* that *all* students face in their learning (see **2**). Inclusive practice is about identifying and removing these barriers, be they physical, psychological, social or cultural. It is also 'about changing the system to fit the student, not the other way around, because the problem of **exclusion** is firmly within the system, not the person or their characteristics' (UNICEF, 2014, p. 18).

It is useful to conceive of inclusive education as forming part of a continuum involving such options as:

1 *exclusion* – students denied access to education for whatever reason;
2 *segregation* – students with individual needs receive education in separate environments designed for them;
3 *differentiation* – students with individual needs placed within mainstream education, the pedagogy accommodates these needs where possible; and
4 *inclusion* – whose educational goal is to respond to all students' needs.

Social justice

Social justice focuses on the need to create a fair society, where everybody has the right to equitable treatment and support, thus enabling everyone to achieve their potential. In the educational context, this requires us to challenge certain structures that perpetuate inequality. Incorporating diverse voices, materials and activities into the curriculum that represent a wide range of cultures and identities is one way of effecting social justice in class. Another strategy is to encourage critical thinking and dialogue. This allows students to develop their own perspectives and become agents of change, even though they may lack privilege outside class. Crucially, we should not impose our own world views on our students, allowing instead their voices to be heard and experiences to be shared (see 5).

Belonging

Students will not be engaged and participate in class if they don't feel they belong there and have a shared purpose. Questions such as: 'Do I get on with the other students?' 'Do the others respect me?' 'Is the teacher fair?' 'Do I get a say in what we do in class?' are ones which students will ask themselves, if only unconsciously. In order for the maximum number of students to answer affirmatively to these questions, it is up to the teacher to create a supportive and trusting environment in class (see C). A **safe space** should always foster a sense of belonging. This should emerge as a result of mutual respect and recognition of similarities and differences within the group.

Intersectionality

This concept is important in inclusive practice as it discourages us from making assumptions about someone based on a single story or characteristic. The term was coined by legal scholar Kimberlé Crenshaw (1989) to describe how different aspects of our identity can interact to shape our experiences and opportunities. Crenshaw talked about how she, as a **Black** woman, faced a particular set of barriers that neither White women nor Black men had to overcome. Intersectionality is thus a way of understanding how multiple forms of inequality or disadvantage can combine and create barriers that may not be commonly appreciated. Intuitively, this makes sense because none of us belongs to one identity category or is defined by one social type. However, I prefer to use the term to refer to all identities and not just those associated with marginalized ones. For example, in **2**, I examine my own identity in detail in terms of my marginalized identities – being Jewish and gay – but, of course, I also possess other 'more privileged' identities. I am cis male, White, middle class and European. Focusing on the marginalized also only tells one side of the story. For example, if a person comes from a wealthy background, they can thrive and enjoy privilege regardless of their otherwise marginalized identities. In practical terms, it is not necessary to know everything about a student, but simply be aware that they will have multiple identities and may suffer different forms of discrimination when these intersect.

Crenshaw, K. (1989) 'Demarginalizing the Intersection of Race and Sex: A Black Feminist Critique of Antidiscrimination Doctrine, Feminist Theory and Antiracist Politics,' *University of Chicago Legal Forum*: Vol. 1989, Article 8. Available at: https://chicagounbound.uchicago.edu/uclf/vol1989/iss1/8

Malone, T. (2022) *The Diversity and Inclusion Glossary.* Pied Wagtail.

OECD (2023) *Equity and Inclusion in Education: Finding Strength through Diversity* (Abridged version), https://www.oecd.org/education/strength-through-diversity/Equity-and-Inclusion-in-Education-abridged-version.pdf, https://doi.org/10.1787/e9072e21-en

UNESCO (2020) *Global Education Monitoring Report: Inclusion and Education: All means All* https://unesdoc.unesco.org/ark:/48223/pf0000373718, https://doi.org/10.54676/JJNK6989

UNICEF (2014) *Conceptualizing Inclusive Education* https://www.unicef.org/eca/sites/unicef.org.eca/files/IE_Webinar_Booklet_1_0.pdf

The concept of barriers is vital to understanding inclusive practice. Barriers prevent us from learning things successfully and we experience them on a regular basis. Identifying them is important, but knowing how they impact learning and how we can overcome them is even more so.

Think of the last time you confused your left with your right, lost your mobile phone or failed to understand a movie plot. These examples may seem trivial, but their familiarity helps us appreciate the multiple barriers we face daily. So how and why do barriers appear? They may be related to our senses (distinguishing left from right), working memory (the mislaid phone), information processing speed (overload of plot detail). They could also be triggered by feelings of stress, low motivation or a lack of confidence or focus. Or we may experience system-wide barriers caused by a difficult learning environment, lack of a digital device or a reliable internet connection (see **17**). There are multiple barriers out there, some of which may be more obvious than others. Stop for a moment to recall barriers that you have experienced while learning something. What kinds of barriers did you experience? Was the barrier related to the activity or the subject itself? Did you lack previous knowledge or a required skill? What was the result of you experiencing this barrier? Did you feel excluded because of it? How could you have overcome the barrier in hindsight?

A personal anecdote

Growing up, I was afraid of water and did not learn to swim along with my peers. I was always in the non-swimmers' group and felt excluded as a result. This stigma worsened as I grew older when I found myself in the same group as far younger students. As a result, I did everything possible to skip these classes and thus exclude myself even more. Looking back, I see now I had very low self-efficacy and this was my main barrier to learning. I was continually telling myself that I would forever be afraid of water and never become a swimmer.

Over-protective parents and my school's policies related to sports (it had a strong academic culture and was less concerned with sports proficiency) allowed me to skip my swimming classes which only reinforced my fear of water. What could the institution or my family have done to remove this barrier? Probably lots of things, but I think one idea could have been to allow me to learn from my peers rather than solely from the instructor (see **13**).

Models and frameworks

With regard to understanding the importance of barriers on our different learners, it is important to look at certain models and frameworks related to identifying and overcoming barriers. The **social model of disability** holds that people with disabilities are **disabled** precisely by *barriers* operating in society that exclude and discriminate against them, not as a result of having the disability in the first place (**the medical model**). These barriers may be physical (e.g. inaccessible toilets), attitudinal (e.g. the idea that disabled people can't be independent), or based around information and communication (e.g. lack of braille options).

The social model is liberating in that it shifts the focus from disabled people (and what they are unable to do) to the disabling world around them. To have the same rights and opportunities as non-disabled people, it is therefore not up to disabled people to change but society.

With regard to frameworks, here are a couple in which the concept of barriers is intrinsic. The first is theoretical in nature referring to the context in which the barriers emerge, the second practical as it explains what to do in class when you have identified a barrier to learning.

Framework 1: The Douglas Fir Group (DFG) (2016) offers us a holistic framework to considering barriers from different perspectives: environmental, societal, organizational or attitudinal. According to this framework, a student may experience barriers to their learning at three different levels:

1 at the *micro* level of social activity (within the home or classroom);
2 at the *meso* level of socio-cultural institutions (within the local community or workplace);
3 at the *macro*-level of ideological structures (linked to society's wider beliefs, as well as cultural, political, economic and religious values and customs).

In my case, for example, the barriers to learning to swim were firmly at the micro and meso levels – directly related to the classroom context, my family and the nature and organization of my school.

Framework 2: Ellis, Kirby and Osborne (2023), within the context of neurodiversity, identify a practical five-step cycle to impactful inclusive practice which can be repeated multiple times in class and is based around overcoming barriers:

Step 1 Identify barriers
Step 2 Focus on the impact of the barrier on learning
Step 3 Remove, reduce and/or rethink the impact of the barrier
Step 4 Embed strategies, evaluate and adjust
Step 5 Transfer/Apply impactful strategies in other contexts.

Let us try and apply this second framework to a language teaching context. Imagine you are giving students a 30-minute timed written exam, but you know from previous experience that the time limit (step 1) will cause some students stress, preventing them from working fast enough to do themselves justice (step 2). As a solution, you could set the test as untimed homework (step 3) and then see if there has been an improvement in results (step 4). Finally, you could then apply this strategy to other contexts such as oral exams or other assessments (step 5) (see **E**). For me, the key point of this cycle is step 2 as 'it focuses on the *impact* of the barrier on learning and the 'interference' it may generate, rather than the cause associated with a specific label' (Ellis, Kirby and Osborne, 2023, p. 85), (see **3**).

Overcoming specific barriers: Talking to the student

It may be that you have a student in class with a specific barrier related to a disability. In an article about teaching students with hearing difficulties, Aldersson (2023) offers some useful advice related to information/communication in the context of teaching deaf students. He suggests first ascertaining how the student identifies in terms of being 'deaf', 'hard of hearing' or as 'someone with hearing loss' (see **3**). If they are a sign language user, and the teacher does not know how to sign, this conversation could be facilitated by an interpreter.

He then outlines five key points to making the learning experience more inclusive for this learner based on the barriers that they might experience:

1 Design classroom seating so that the student can see you and each other clearly.
2 Make sure the classroom is well-lit to facilitate speech-reading.
3 Use captions or transcripts where possible or voice recognition software on the student's device.
4 Speak normally but clearly and try not to exaggerate your mouth patterns.
5 Try to keep background noise to a minimum (for those using hearing aids).

His main point is to talk to the students concerned preferably before the first class to ascertain what their needs and preferences are – for example, where they would like to sit and how they can best access the content. Asking such questions about a student's life experience is always important as the more you know, the more barriers you can identify and, in time, help remove. The crucial thing is to think ahead, anticipate **accommodations** and plan for as many potential barriers as possible.

Aldersson, R. (2023) 'An inclusive approach to teaching English to deaf adult learners,' in Hunter, A. M. (Ed.) *Diversity and Inclusion in English Language Education.* Routledge.

Douglas Fir Group. (2016) A transdisciplinary framework for SLA in a multilingual world. *Modern Language Journal*, 100 (Supplement 2016) https://doi.org/10.1111/modl.12301

Ellis, P. Kirby, A. and Osborne, A. (2023) *Neurodiversity and Education.* Corwin.

3   Reframing labels

> We are surrounded by labels and the language classroom
> is no exception. Think of the ways we label our students
> according to background, age, proficiency, disability,
> ethnicity, etc. We are so accustomed to labels that we
> rarely stop to consider their connotations and the often
> negative impact they may have.

A common error is to read up on the latest labels and terms and, when
faced by a particular student in class, rush to classify them. This is
never a good idea. It is always preferable to attempt to understand the
person before attaching a label. An important consideration, therefore,
when ensuring inclusion, is to be particularly sensitive about the use of
labels and to strive for them to have a positive impact if and when used.
Ironically, some such labels (such as BIPOC) are coined to describe
marginalized groups but their use can be counterproductive, limiting
and stigmatizing identities in a similar way as conventional labels do.
See 30 for a critical look at labels used in inclusive practice.

Reframing labels

When I first started researching inclusion in language teaching, I noticed
how much the term was primarily associated with students with **SEN**
(Special Educational Needs). This struck me as an incongruous acronym
because, to my mind, it reinforces **medical model** thinking, and may
blur our understanding of a student's disabilities. The word 'special'
also suggests students require special attention and that teachers have
to be specially trained to teach them effectively. The label is also rather
disempowering as it focuses on the services required by these students
instead of the people and the community to which they belong. As
such, the label may contribute to marginalization. For this reason,
the labels SEN or SEND (D for **disability**) are gradually becoming
redundant as inclusive teaching now focuses on pedagogical practices
which all students will benefit from. In fact, **neurodiverse** has, in many

circles, replaced SEN as the adjective to describe students with specific cognitive learning differences such as **autism**, **ADHD** or dyslexia. Not being an acronym, it also feels less like a label. However, it is worth pointing out that the term *neurodiversity*, according to The Brain Charity (2022), is 'most commonly now used to refer to a group which encompasses the full spectrum of brain differences and is made up of both **neurodivergent** and **neurotypical** individuals.'

Within the umbrella term *neurodiversity*, of course other labels are frequently used. Let us consider ADHD which stands for *attention deficit hyperactivity disorder*. It would be hard to think of a more negative sounding label as it suggests a person with a 'disordered' brain (compared to a 'normal' one) which may lead to a 'wrong' kind of behaviour. But, as with SEN, such labels are now starting to be critiqued. Indeed, Ellis et al. (2023, p. 65) suggest reframing the ADHD label so that it does not imply people who 'do not attend' but rather those who 'attend to everything' and 'hyper-focus'. This reframing is significant because it 'shifts our attention from the label or presentation of a diagnosis to the *lived experience* (my italics) which, in turn, will shape the strategies and interventions we put in place to support a learner.' This reframing also highlights the strengths that people with ADHD may possess such as making connections that go unnoticed by others or working well to deadlines. For example, Aherne (2023) refers to the fact that many paramedics have ADHD as the high-pressure conditions of their work suits their combination of hyper-focus and super-fast processing.

Another label often used in relation to inclusive practices is students with SEBD (social, emotional and behavioural difficulties). Like ADHD, it is a deficit label with 'difficulty' having a similar effect to 'disorder'. As with SEN, I have preferred not to use this term because of its stigmatizing effect. However, you will still see it used in multiple contexts, as is SEN. Many students do, of course, face difficulties and disadvantages due to displacement and trauma, as well as socio-economic or cultural factors, but I don't feel attaching a generic label to describe them is helpful. There is also the risk of a label of this kind becoming a self-fulfilling prophecy (see **11**).

Labels and identity

Labels are intrinsically bound up with one's sense of self. It is therefore important to listen to the learner and respect the label they prefer to use, if any. For example, in the case of neurodiversity, some people welcome the label that a diagnosis provides because it gives a feeling of relief ('So now I know why I'm like this') and opens up the chance to belong to a community. While others reject such a medical label ('I can't identify with this condition at all').

Importantly, a distinction can also be made between labelling oneself using *person first language* (e.g. 'a person with autism') or *identity first language* (e.g. 'an autistic person'). By foregrounding the individual, 'person first' language suggests that disability status – one's autism (in this case) – does not define who one is. By contrast, identity first language suggests that the description (autism) forms a core part of one's sense of self. People who use identity first language don't feel that their disability negates or takes anything away from their identity. Either description is likely to be empowering to the individual, depending on how they identify. Accepting or rejecting a label to describe oneself is an intensely personal choice.

Takeaways

Resist labels which stigmatize or connote a deficit based on a societal **norm**. These may not be apparently obvious as they do not need to relate to a particular marginalized group (e.g. 'false beginner'). Consider rather the individual's lived experience. If applying a label, try to choose one that will have a positive impact and do not allow it to hide an individual's strengths.

The use of labels is in constant flux (see **Glossary**). Old labels get reframed, critiqued and new ones come along to replace them. This reframing usually highlights changes in the way inclusive practice is considered. However, labels can also re-emerge when reclaimed by a community, such as the label *queer* which was a highly pejorative term but now forms part of the **LGBTQIA+** acronym (lesbian, gay, bisexual, **transgender**, queer, intersex and asexual people) (see **6**).

Challenging the differences between labels (e.g. that between dyslexia and ADHD) can allow us to focus more on *impact on learning*. Doing so may help us identify patterns common to many individuals rather than those belonging to a single group. Labels are intrinsically personal. Some students may feel empowered by being part of a community while others will reject such a label. As with pronoun choice, allow the student to describe their preferred label or how they wish to be called and follow their lead.

Aherne, D. (2023) *The Pocket Guide to Neurodiversity*. London: Jessica Kingsley.

Ellis, P., Kirby, A. and Osborne, A. (2023) *Neurodiversity and Education*. Corwin.

The Brain Charity (2022) https://www.thebraincharity.org.uk/neurodivergent-neurodiversity-neurotypical-explained/

4 Identity and life experience

> To describe identity, we can use the following categories: ethnicity, religion, sexual orientation, gender identity, age, ability, socioeconomic status, nationality, citizenship status and linguistic identity.

Indeed, there are a lot of aspects that contribute to our sense of self, and some may be more important to you than others. How you rank these aspects goes to make up your personal identity (how you perceive yourself). However, these aspects will also emerge in the way you present yourself to others, for example, using particular logos or symbols to project your identity in social media. This is our social identity; it communicates how we wish to be perceived and is linked to our sense of belonging and affinity with others. It is important to stress here one's *sense of affiliation or affinity*. If you feel this towards a particular group, it may mean that you feel a great sense of trust and belonging with this group and seek them out. As Norton (2013, p. 47) has said, 'I take the position that identity references desire – the desire for recognition, the desire for affiliation, and the desire for security and safety.'

Reflecting on identity is important because how we see ourselves has a big influence on how we work and the attitudes that we bring to class. Our experience of the world also impacts on our classroom practice, as does the marginalization and **discrimination** that we may have faced in our lives or seen others face close at hand. There is a strong connection here between our identity and that of others and intercultural awareness which Byram (1997, p. 34) defined as: 'knowledge of others; knowledge of self; skills to interpret and relate; skills to discover and/or to interact; valuing others' values, beliefs, and behaviours; and relativizing one's self.'

The questions below are for you to reflect on and answer individually. You could also ask your students some of these questions or get them to ask each other similar ones. However, this would require a supportive and trusting atmosphere in class as some questions are, of course, highly personal. Always be wary of forcing students to reveal information about themselves and their lives which may be triggering (cause painful emotions). It may simply be enough to get students to reflect on these questions and write down their experiences individually and for their reference only. So, to give you an idea, here is how I would choose to represent myself both in terms of my **marginalized** identities (being gay and Jewish) and my non-marginalized identities (White, cis male, middle class, etc.). For inclusive practice, it is important to refer to both as we should be interested in what we share as a *community* not just what separates us (see 30). Therefore, the more identities and affinities you can refer to the better, as you will have a greater chance of being able to find common ground with others.

At the end, I also detail my experience of others who feel marginalized. This is important because such experiences impact on what we consider as 'usual' in society.

Who are you according to these ten categories?

Ethnicity: White, British, great grandparents of Polish and Lithuanian origin
Religion: Jewish
Sexual orientation: gay
Gender identity: cis male
Age: middle aged
Ability: **neurotypical**
Socioeconomic status: university educated, middle class
Nationality: British
Citizenship: resident in Spain since 1991
Languages: English, Spanish, Portuguese, Catalan

How would you briefly describe your background/life experience?

I grew up in North London in the UK and had a very liberal upbringing. My parents sent me to a state school which brought me into contact with many students of different ethnicities and socioeconomic backgrounds as the catchment area of the school covered a very broad cross-section of the city's population. There was also a good percentage of Jewish students, so that we had our own assemblies. Unlike many teenagers, I also had classmates who were gay, something which I think was unheard of during the 1980s.

Have you ever suffered discrimination and/or marginalization? How has this affected your identity?

I experienced a degree of discrimination particularly as a young gay man growing up in the UK but that has not impacted me as much as some of my peers. Although I was born in 1966 and grew up with Section 28 (Section 28 took effect from 1988 and banned the promotion of homosexuality by local authorities. This legislation was not repealed until 2003 in England and Wales), I didn't have great problems coming out and always had a supportive network of friends and family. Perhaps because I didn't have to fight that hard to defend my gay identity, I don't think of it as being central to my sense of self and it is not something I consciously project to others. I have encountered antisemitism at different times of my life but more so in recent years as a result of comments and messages posted in social media. The people sending these messages do not know me and the comments are often anonymous. Because my surname marks my Jewish identity very clearly, I sense that I suffer this more than some of my contemporaries. Many Jews change their surnames for this reason, of course. I'm not a practising Jew – I don't read Hebrew or go to synagogue or even feel a strong spiritual link with Judaism – but I do feel a strong affiliation with other Jews as well as Jewish culture, festivals, celebrations and cuisine. I try to maintain some of these things in my life and that helps me retain a connection with my roots.

Have you had any close-hand experience of other marginalized identities? If so, give one example and explain how this affected you.

I see my brother-in-law regularly. He has muscular dystrophy from birth. Spending time with him has made me much more conscious of the needs of wheelchair users in general, particularly when travelling or in unfamiliar situations. Due to the time that we have spent together, I am conscious of people's different attitudes to him. Many people we come across are open and helpful but many others stare, feel uncomfortable around him, lower their gaze or simply walk away. As in many modern cities, accessibility has improved a good deal in Barcelona where we live, but there is still a long way to go, and I am acutely aware of this.

Takeaway task

'**Your Names**'. Students think of all the different names or titles that they have in different contexts and ask and answer questions about them in pairs. For example, *I'm Ben, but on my passport, it says Benjamin. My grandma called me Benjy, she was the only one. Some friends now call me Benito, but I don't like it. In Argentina, they called me Bencito. In some universities, they call me Dr. Goldstein, but I'm not a doctor or have a PhD.* As a variation, this task works nicely with images of yourself in different contexts. Students can show these images with the different names and their partners have to match them to create their distinct identities.

Byram, M. (1997) *Teaching and Assessing Intercultural Communicative Competence*. Multilingual Matters.

Norton, B. (2013) *Identity and Language Learning, Extending the Conversation*. Multilingual Matters.

5 Critical pedagogy and inclusive practice

Our political and social systems often reflect what is referred to as *the dominant culture*. In much of the world, that culture can be identified as male, White and middle class. Let's look at how challenging the dominant culture lies at the heart of both inclusion and critical pedagogy.

The Brazilian educational theorist Paulo Freire (1970) was one of the first to recognize that educational systems benefited children from a dominant and privileged culture. These children progressed because they understood the system and saw themselves reflected in it, while children from poorer families had the opposite experience. And, of course, the same thing happens today, although we may not always be aware of the process. Indeed, the values associated with dominant cultures often become so entrenched in society that they cease to be as visible as the inequalities faced by those who remain outside of that culture.

Critical pedagogy focuses on addressing these social inequalities and power imbalances in education. It encourages educators to examine and challenge the dominant culture's oppressive structures to foster social justice and equity (see **1**). Crucially, critical pedagogy has an action orientation approach, of which a key concept is 'critical consciousness' or, as Freire (1970) referred to it in Portuguese, *conscientização* – referring to the ability to see what is wrong with society and the willingness to do something about it. This is achieved by developing a methodology based on disruption, on questioning assumptions and problem-posing. Freire claimed that teachers could best arrive at this via a problematizing dialogue with students. This dialogue would identify barriers faced by them or others in society and work towards developing actions that address these problems, both inside and outside the classroom. It also creates a more equal relationship between teacher and student. As Freire (1970, p. 80) himself put it: 'The teacher is no longer merely the one who teaches, but one who is himself (sic) taught in dialogue with the student, who in turn while being taught, also teaches.'

Connections

Reading the above, you may be able to see how there exist strong parallels between critical pedagogy and inclusive practice. One of the strongest connections is this focus on student-centredness. In both approaches, learners actively participate in the learning process, contributing to a more democratic and collaborative classroom environment (see **C**). Both concepts also foster students' sense of agency and encourage them to challenge and analyse societal **norms** and structures. Indeed, similar questions could be posed in both approaches. For example, the questions below could be asked in a wide range of contexts from an analysis of language teaching materials (see **D**) to that of an entire school's organization (see **F**) and beyond:

- Who has power and agency?
- Who has less or none? Why?
- Who or what is included?
- Who or what has been erased or **marginalized**?
- What assumptions are being made?
- How are students positioned?
- In whose interests am I / is the material / is the school acting?

Importantly, both critical pedagogy and inclusive education navigate socio-political issues. Perhaps, because of this, proponents of both often refer to their work as an 'everyday struggle' against the forces of a dominant culture. For this reason, it can often prove unpredictable and frustrating. However hard it may be to convince others of your position, the fight should remain a political one.

In this respect, both practices demand great *criticality* and a *call for action*. This is particularly true when inclusive education is at its most disruptive. It is not just about thinking or reflecting on society but creating the potential to act within it and make a difference.

The three Ps: Power, privilege and positionality

To help you incorporate some ideas of critical pedagogy in class, it is worth reflecting on yourself and what action you can take to make a difference. The following questions are focused on power:

- What is within your realm of influence to change? How can you leverage your power and privilege to enact positive change?
- Who is impacted by the decisions you make?
- What do you *not* have control over that you need to accept in order to move forward?

You can also ask yourself similar questions with regard to your **positionality**. This can be done practically by way of a statement, which is how you would describe your social identity, but with specific reference to a particular branch of your work. You can create this on your own or with colleagues. Doing so may be a good way to explore how your values impact on your worldview. It may also reveal certain **biases** and privileges you may hold (see **11**). Sharing positionality statements is a great way to build trust and show learners the values that you apply to your teaching practice. For example:

My teaching philosophy is rooted in the belief that learning a language is not just about communication but deeper cultural understanding and personal growth. My approach is student-centred and I prioritize critical thinking and positive interaction in my classroom practice.

Students can also share their statements and answer questions about them afterwards, for example:

1 What did you learn about yourself and your partner?
2 How are your positionality statements similar/different?
3 What does this reveal about identity and privilege?
4 Why is it important to recognize identities and privilege?

Certain privileges that you hold may emerge in the positionality statement, but you can focus on these specifically by doing a '*privilege walk*' in class. Note: Only do this is in a face-to-face classroom setting if you believe a safe learning environment (see **C**) has been established and students feel a high level of trust with you and amongst themselves.

Task instructions: Participants stand along a line in the middle of the room and the teacher reads a series of statements. The students step forwards (SF) or backwards (SB) depending on whether the statement represents a privilege for them or not. Sample statements could be:

- If you feel comfortable walking home alone at night (SF/+1)
- If you have been stopped by the police because they believed you were suspicious (SB/-1)
- If you get time off for religious holidays (SF/+1)
- If you were bullied or made fun of at school (SB/-1)
- If you have ever been told you should talk differently to fit in or gain credibility (SB/-1)
- If you studied the culture or history of your ancestors at school (SF/+1)

Depending on students' replies, they will end up in different places in the room. Alternatively, you can do this in a virtual environment, using numbers which the students keep in their minds rather than physical steps, (i.e. one step forward = +1, one step back = -1). This may work better because, in the physical classroom, those students with less privilege are required to share this amongst their classmates – something which might make them feel uncomfortable. Finally, remember students should not feel they have to share their answers with others if they do not wish to.

Freire, P. (1970, 2000) *The Pedagogy of the Oppressed*. (30th Anniversary Edition). Continuum.

6   Using inclusive language

> This idea looks at the importance of using inclusive language and discusses three particular areas of interest. Please read this in conjunction with the Glossary and 3 on labels to gain a broader view of inclusive language.

The first thing to remember about inclusive language is that the terms used are in constant flux and can change rapidly. Their meaning and associations can also vary enormously from place to place. For that reason, it is important when speaking in international contexts that you do not take for granted language or **norms** that are specific to a certain culture or discourse. Essentially, this focus on language is not just about using the right or the wrong term, it is rather about how language shapes identities, and reinforces or deconstructs systems of power that maintain inequality. For this reason, rather than simply list certain preferred terms which you will find in a hundred EDIB language guideline documents, I wanted to devote an idea to looking at a couple of terms in a critical and more in-depth way. Such an analysis could be done with virtually any of the terms you'll find in this book. Remember – if in doubt about which term to use, it is important to adhere to the basic principles of inclusive language and *call people what they call themselves*.

Race/Ethnicity: Black

When it comes to inclusive language, one of the most complex areas is **race** and **ethnicity**. Indeed, before looking at the term *Black* specifically, we need to distinguish between the two previous terms and unpack them. *Race* is a social construct used to categorize people based on perceived physical traits (e.g. skin colour). As Stollznow (2020, p. 12) has said: 'Even though there is no scientific basis for the theories or ideologies of race, it remains a proxy or general term for categorization, although it is often replaced by less emotionally charged terms such as people(s), population …'

Ethnicity, however, is a term used to describe a social group with a shared cultural identity and/or common ancestry. Neither are biological categories, and *race* has become a discredited term as its use maintains a socio-political hierarchy. Despite this, the term *race* remains ubiquitous even in inclusive language guides – often because of the need to critique it!

Within this category, you will hear a number of different acronyms such as POC (**People of Colour**) or **BIPOC** (Black, **Indigenous**, People of Colour). However, I feel these acronyms are unhelpful as they imply that people belong to one homogeneous group. As the American Psychological Association (APA) guide (2023, p. 22) says: '… some terms or phrases that were initially created to encourage solidarity among different racial movements may over time become descriptors that erase distinctions.'

Most inclusive language guides then suggest that *Black* should be written with a capital *B*. The argument in support of capitalization is that it is more than just a colour descriptor but refers to a specific identity and community, similar to the way that *Asian* is capitalized. It is also seen as a sign of respect and empowerment, recognizing the cultural contributions and histories of Black people and countering historically negative and oppressive stereotypes (see **22**).

However, like so much inclusive terminology, not everybody agrees. Dabiri (2021, pp. 65–66) says arguing over capital letters distracts from more important questions: 'the capital B – while coming from a place that understandably is attempting to confer more status on to the word 'black' – seeks to reinforce a way of seeing the world that we should be disrupting and unravelling.' Indeed, it is revealing in her book that she frequently places *Black* and *White* in inverted commas, 'intentionally disrupting the comfort with which we rely on that terminology' (ibid).

I agree with Dabiri and my take on it is if Black is capitalized then so should **White** and **Whiteness** for that matter. Another problem with the term *People of Colour* is that it suggests that there are people *without* colour (i.e. White people) who represent the default and are simply 'people'. For this reason, *Whiteness*, if not capitalized, should also be named, so White people are also viewed as a category.

Sexual orientation: Queer

Originally a highly pejorative and insulting term, *queer* has been
reclaimed by some in the LGBTQIA+ community as an 'umbrella
term to describe someone who does not conform to socialized gender
norms' (Seburn, 2021, p. 98). Indeed, it is represented by the *Q* in
the above acronym which has granted the term far greater exposure.
Some people use *queer* because they want to show their membership
of the community without specifying any further information about
themselves. Others may use it if they have more than one identity (e.g.
bisexual and **non-binary**). The term's lack of definition is important,
indeed *queer* is frequently used to refer generally to non-conventional
lifestyle choices. You may hear the term *queer culture*, for example.
You will also find it used frequently in academic contexts: *queer
theory* refers to study and research that challenges or subverts
heteronormativity. In this context, you may also hear the word used as
a verb: *to queer the coursebook*, for example, meaning to disrupt its
heteronormative approach. However, although *queer* was reclaimed
in the 1990s, the term can still have negative connotations for some
people, and it is not a universally accepted term within the LGBTQIA+
community today. As always, ask people how they self-identify before
labelling their sexual orientation.

Gender: Personal pronouns

It has become common practice to identify yourself with your pronouns
(subject and/or possessives) in brackets as part of a social media profile
or email signature or when introducing yourself. This is good practice as
it prevents us making assumptions about a person's gender and putting
the onus on people to correct those assumptions. Some people choose
to place their pronouns in other languages first to challenge English's
status as the world's lingua franca (see **10**). This is particularly common
when the person speaks multiple languages. In my case, this would be
'Ben Goldstein *(él/ell/ele/he)*' – indicating Spanish/Catalan/Portuguese
and English in the last place.

Pronoun etiquette

When referring to personal pronouns, some people choose to avoid
the term *preferred* as this assumes that a person has made a choice:

identified pronouns or simply *pronouns* should suffice (e.g. 'Which pronouns do you use?'). When referring to someone you know, use that person's identified pronouns. This is a way to respect them just as using or pronouncing a person's name correctly (see **9, 11**).

When describing a person whose identified pronouns are not known or when their gender is irrelevant in a particular context, use the singular 'they' to avoid making assumptions. It is quite usual to use 'they' in such cases rather than 'he/she', e.g. in 'Who is your favourite singer? Why are *they* your favourite?'

During group introductions, you can invite people to share their pronouns if they are comfortable but insist that there is no obligation. Start by saying 'I use x/x pronouns,' rather than 'I use female/male pronouns,' (again to avoid the binary where possible).

American Psychological Association (2023) *Inclusive Language Guide* (2nd Ed.) https://www.apa.org/about/apa/equity-diversity-inclusion/language-guidelines.pdf

Dabiri, E. (2021) *What White People Can Do Next: From Allyship to Coalition.* Penguin.

Oxfam (2023) *Inclusive Language Guide.* Retrievable at: https://policy-practice.oxfam.org/resources/inclusive-language-guide-621487/

Seburn, T. (2021) *How to Write Inclusive ELT materials.* Teacher 2 Writer.

Stollznow, K. (2020) *On the Offensive: Prejudice in Language Past and Present.* Cambridge University Press.

B: Methodology: Strategies and activities

Making sure all students feel they belong in class requires teachers to possess both classroom management and interpersonal skills. It is fundamentally about taking an interest in our students as people and understanding what they need to best achieve their objectives.

Thanks to Paulo Dantas for his help with **12**.

Barriers to learning can be multi-faceted – physical, cognitive or cultural (see **2**) – so there are many strategies and interventions available to counter them. Here we look at different ways that lesson design and delivery can help in this endeavour.

The **Universal Design** for Learning (UDL) (CAST, 2024) is a useful framework for developing lesson plans, activities, resources and assessments. It can be helpful for multiple students who need adaptations to be able to engage and participate actively in class, but it also has specific applications for **neurodiverse** students and those with disabilities. Remember that specialist knowledge is not required to carry out these strategies and interventions and that they apply to all good teaching and learning, not just inclusive practice. In fact, you may already carry out some of them in class.

The UDL Framework is based on three main principles (see also **24**):

Engagement – the 'why' of learning – the ways we motivate our learners and sustain their interest. For example, providing clear aims so learning outcomes are clear or designing seating in a way to encourage interaction.

Representation – the 'what' of learning – the ways we provide data in different formats, depending on student needs, for example, using images to support the use of verbal or written instructions.

Action and expression – the 'how' of learning – the ways students will demonstrate their learning and understanding to others and for themselves, for example, preferring to make a video for their assignment rather than write a text (see **8**).

We can use this framework to help make adjustments both to the design of our classes and to how we deliver them. As in many other areas of inclusive practice, it requires us to build in choice and flexibility to accommodate all students and, where possible, to plan these interventions in advance.

Design: The physical and sensory environment

It is not possible to create perfect conditions for everyone in the classroom, but student engagement and focus can be boosted by both cognitive and physical comfort. Scrivener (2012) details five different considerations with regard to the physical environment: light, acoustics, noise, ventilation and temperature. Of course, some of these things will be beyond your control to adjust but it is worth bearing in mind that light, noise or disturbance from other students are sensory triggers for neurodiverse students and affect their emotional well-being. For example, it may be a good idea to minimize distraction by seating students away from windows if they are likely to get over stimulated. Consider also whether visual cues and support, such as posters and charts on walls, focus or distract the learners. Alternatively, providing individual quiet, working time places for easily distracted students is a good choice if you have the option.

As for whole class seating, an informal semi-circle or a tipped-U design (if you need desk space) will encourage student interaction. Consider peer learning (see **13**) and how students will interact (in pairs, small or large groups) when designing seating plans – flexibility and the ability to move furniture around is clearly an advantage here. Bear in mind both class work and other aspects of the school environment (e.g. break or lunch time). Simple approaches such as having consistent seating plans can help reduce the risk of anxiety or distraction for some learners. If you are going to make changes, let students know beforehand along with any other changes to the class routine.

In terms of students with physical disability, it is common sense to keep aisles and floors clear and for them to feel as comfortable as possible. Be mindful that all students should be able to see and hear as clearly as possible and to interact with other students with ease.

Delivery: Instructions and descriptions

With regard to *representation*, bear in mind some neurodiverse students may have difficulty with retaining information, understanding instructions or the complexities of language used. To alleviate this, provide instructions in multimodal formats where possible (using bullet points, visuals, audio, etc.). In particular, a simple image can help students to process, retain and recall knowledge. With written descriptions, asking learners to underline the key words of rubrics and then repeating them back to you is a good way to check they have captured instructions correctly.

With spoken descriptions, consider differentiating language and instructions as a routine part of your practice, e.g. be succinct, use simpler language, slow down delivery, stress key words and again use visuals or body language to support understanding. With regard to discipline, use non-verbal cues and signals to keep noise down and distractions and stress to a minimum.

When introducing new ideas (e.g. cultural input in a text), breaking down information into manageable chunks can be effective and boost students' ability to process, organize and recall it. You can do this by providing short and simple summaries as you go. This helps learners reinforce prior knowledge and provide context. Students can return to them to consolidate their learning. These can be designed in the form of mind maps or other types of graphic organizers to aid memorization. Similarly, breaking down reading texts into smaller parts and asking questions after each part is another useful strategy to improve comprehension.

Allowing additional processing time for students to answer questions and understand descriptions and instructions is another vital element of inclusive practice. Giving students extra time to double-check their answers is also very helpful.

Learning outcomes

With regard to the UDL's final principle, *Action and expression*, it is important to state the learning outcomes at the start of the lesson and the choices available to students to achieve them (see 8). Ensuring that these are understood and referred to regularly may help focus learner attention. Reviewing and summarizing learning outcomes will help learners see if their personal learning targets have been achieved which will give them a sense of progress.

Finally, it is important to introduce these interventions and strategies little by little. Take the time to support the students to make their own choices and develop their own learning strategies. Giving students enough time and space to do this is essential, as it is more likely that learners will make cumulative gains in their learning rather than sudden great leaps.

Here, the focus has been primarily on external factors (learning environment, pace, content and aims of the materials, learning objectives, etc.) but consider also strategies and interventions related to internal factors (well-being, anxiety and self-confidence). For example, one strategy is to set tasks with easy success rates before setting more demanding ones: this can allow you to praise students and thus enhance their self-esteem.

CAST (2024) *Universal Design for Learning Guidelines version 3.0.* Retrieved from https://udlguidelines.cast.org

Scrivener, J. (2012) *Classroom Management Techniques.* Cambridge University Press.

Offering choice

> To create a more inclusive learning environment, students must be involved in making choices and decisions about their own learning. By doing this, they are sharing responsibilities and making the whole experience more engaging and motivating.

It is not always possible to offer learners choice because of logistics, time constraints or because the institution where you work may not fully appreciate the benefit of doing so. For that reason, this section gives practical suggestions that won't put you under too much strain. Finally, do not assume that because a student belongs to a certain **marginalized** group, they will prefer a particular way of doing things. It is always better to listen to your learners and find out their preferences directly from them.

It may also not be easy to offer choice from the outset. For example, in the case of materials for dyslexic students, certain colours, fonts and layouts will be easier to navigate than others. However, once you have established these adjustments, it is then good practice to offer them to all students and allow them to choose. This avoids singling out students in a very public way.

As a general rule, it is a good idea to offer choice gradually. Mercer and Puchta (2023, p. 40) recommend an approach which 'starts with giving students easy options concerning the *how* of their learning first, and the *what* later. Trying to change too much too fast may indeed lead to frustration.'

Here are some areas where it is relatively easy to offer choice:

Seating arrangements

Allow students to choose where they would like to sit in class, taking into account factors like sensory needs, social preferences or learning focus (see 7).

Student projects and presentations

Rather than dictate a particular format for a project or presentation, allow students to declare a preference from a menu of choices. For example, this could be in the form of an illustrated essay, a poster, a video or a slideshow with a written or spoken commentary. Students can do the project individually or with a supportive peer. Clearly, the preference will be related to learner difference so, for those who find writing challenging, visual media here will be a logical choice. Students may not know which format they prefer, so before they make a choice it is generally a good idea to show different models from previous students. Once they have seen such examples, they should be able to perceive the differences and which skills each format requires. You could offer templates and frameworks for these projects and presentations which would save time for both you and the students.

Student roles

When doing collaborative tasks, make sure the task requires clearly delineated roles and allow students to choose the role that they would prefer. For example, imagine that the students' task is to create a promotional campaign for a certain product. Students might be able to select their role from researcher, organizer, transcriber and spokesperson (see **9**). Each role may play to a student's individual strengths. For example, the researcher may be good at selecting and filtering information, the organizer at creating mind maps and prioritizing the information to include, the transcriber at recording every person's point of view, the spokesperson at articulating the group's ideas. If there is a student with particular skills or knowledge that is related to the theme of the project, make sure that their group and others know it. This person could become an expert or consultant.

Responses to text

We are used to presenting students with texts and giving them all the same response options but if they are offered choice then it's more likely that they will respond more enthusiastically and effectively. Start with two options at first and then move on to offering further ones. For example, depending on your age group and level, the different responses to a short story could be:

- Put the pictures of the story in order
- Describe a personal connection to it
- Create a (different) book cover for it
- Summarize its main points
- Act out a scene from it
- Change its genre and so on.

The advantage of offering these choices is that students may well go for very different options. This means that when they come to compare their responses, they are able to gain a multi-layered or 'big picture' appreciation of the text in question.

Choice boards

Choice boards show a set of different tasks which students can select as they please. They can work very well for young learners. For example, imagine you are asking your group to discuss favourite hobbies and interests. They can select from these different options: make a poster, make a recording, interview a friend about the topic, write from the perspective of another person (e.g. celebrity), etc. It is important to vary these as much as you can both in terms of difficulty level, range of skills and media and collaboration (working individually or in pairs). Even though some tasks may be more challenging, they must all be evaluated equally. Finally, it is important to give the students sufficient time to reflect on the different tasks on the board and discuss them amongst themselves if necessary. This is important to prevent students being swayed by their peers. Once the class gets used to working with choice boards, you can get your students to create their own ones. This will undoubtedly increase their engagement and motivation.

Goals or learning targets

Your curriculum will probably dictate the official learning goals or targets but, in addition to this, it is always worth asking learners to identify what is important to their learning and find out what their individual or group goals are. They may be able to achieve these specifically in tasks which give them more flexibility and choice such as project work.

Mercer, S. and Puchta, H. (2023) *101 Psychological Tips*. Cambridge University Press & Assessment.

A positive consequence of the COVID pandemic was a greater focus on trust, well-being and acceptance. In addition, many teachers were able to reach out to their students and make positive connections which led to greater participation and interaction.

For an inclusive class environment to flourish, students should be accepting of all members' identities. As Carl Rogers (1983, p. 124) noted: '[Acceptance] is prizing the learner, prizing her (sic) feelings, her opinions, her person … It is an acceptance of this other individual as a separate person, having worth in their own right.'

This sentiment echoes the principles of positive psychology which focuses not only on promoting personal growth but also on contributing to the well-being of others. If students are in a safe environment and trusting of their peers, this will lead to greater engagement and thus greater participation and interaction, a defining characteristic of the inclusive classroom.

Here are some ways to accentuate the positive and thus maximize participation and interaction in class:

Maintaining a positive attitude

This can be as simple as greeting students and remembering their names. Good behaviour should also be noticed and commented on publicly, as this can motivate and create a positive attitude. As Sowton (2021, p. 176) says: 'These behaviours do not necessarily need to be big – e.g. 'Juan, I liked how quickly and nicely you formed your groups'… (but) there is a particular power if you name the student, as others will also want to be named.' Messages such as these need not even be a sentence, they may only consist of single word, gesture or a facial expression but accumulatively, they can have a very positive effect on your students' well-being and self-esteem.

Developing a group dynamic

To create positive group dynamics and develop greater trust and acceptance, we should aim for all students to develop some kind of personal relationship with each other (see **13**). However, this is not always easy as students often prefer to choose their own partner or group, especially at the outset of a course. One way to pre-empt this is to give the class short and easy tasks such as warmers or icebreakers that they have to do with new partners so they do not feel threatened. Alternatively, set up more random groupings (e.g. 'Work with someone who was born in the same month as you') rather than explicitly set up new groups. These accidental groups are effective as they add an element of fun and surprise. Strategies such as these help the group to gel as all students will get to know each other to a certain extent.

Giving thoughtful feedback

It is easy during lessons to focus on errors and miss positive contributions, but learners need to know when they have done something well. If the feedback is public, it can benefit both the individual student and others in class, who will have their attention drawn to, say, a particular language point used well. Indeed, the most effective forms of praise are specific (e.g. 'I really liked the way you emphasized that word. It really helped you get your message across'). Generally speaking, relate feedback to clear and concrete goals so that the student can process it easily.

Modelling respect

This is a key way to establish positive relationships in class and can be achieved simply by smiling, nodding and modelling the use of polite language and good manners (use of 'please' and 'thank you'). It is also a good idea to learn something about each student or, at the very least, remember basic information about them (e.g. their background, their tastes, etc.). As Mercer and Puchta (2023, p. 27) say, 'these bits of information are like social-emotional jewels – when learners notice you remember them, they will feel appreciated, included and will be more likely to engage positively.'

Letting students see their progress

Language learning can be slow and progress imperceptible at times. The CEFR's 'can do' statements break down communicative competence into more manageable objectives and they have now become ubiquitous in our teaching materials as a form of self-assessment. However, they often only focus on what a student can or can't do at a given moment. But how does a student know this for sure? It is more helpful if these statements are nuanced and allow for some kind of ambiguity, emotional response or contextual information. This can be achieved by simply tweaking the sentence stems in the self-assessment charts (e.g. 'I still need to work on …, … but I'm improving with …', 'In class today, I was able to … for the first time', etc.). Such self-reflection can have a positive impact on student engagement and interaction because it allows students to notice patterns in the learning process.

Avoiding interaction bias

Mercer and Dörnyei (2020, p. 27) mention that involving all students is a defining characteristic of the inclusive classroom. The teacher's role is all important here: 'teachers need not only to attend to how they model inclusion in their treatment of all learners in class, but also to take note of which learners may be excluded by their peers and find ways to consciously ensure they are included.' For this reason, it is a good idea to focus on how you interact with your class and avoid any kind of interaction **bias,** such as always turning to the same students – often those who are the most assertive – to elicit responses (see **11**). Sadly, many students' lack of participation is caused by their teacher not addressing them explicitly. A teacher's interaction bias may be verbal or shown by body language, eye contact or gesture. If you have the chance to observe another teacher, it is a good practice to pay attention to these 'attending strategies' such as smiling, nodding, using the student's name and so on and draw conclusions from the analysis (see Wajnryb, 1992).

Listening to students

It is well known that attentive listening not only demonstrates respect for others but expands the range and depth of communication. Conversation on a more profound level implies being open, sharing common ground or learning from your students. This may mean reassessing your role to become more of a coach or a facilitator to others' communication. In order to do this, try to be patient and allow students sufficient time to respond as they will need to reflect on what they want to say.

Mercer, S. and Dörnyei, Z. (2020) *Engaging Language Learners in Contemporary Classrooms*. Cambridge University Press & Assessment.

Mercer, S. and Puchta, H. (2023) *101 Psychological Tips*. Cambridge University Press & Assessment.

Rogers, C. (1983) *Freedom to Learn for the 80s*. Merril.

Sowton, C. (2021) *Teaching in Challenging Circumstances*. Cambridge University Press & Assessment.

Wajnryb, R. (1992) *Classroom Observation Tasks: A Resource Book for Language Teachers and Trainers*. Cambridge University Press.

Using and respecting learners' own language

Using the students' own language is still considered by many teachers as an obstacle to the studying of a second or an additional language. However, it is now increasingly thought of as a useful tool and an important way to empower learners.

When I first started teaching in the early 1990s in Spain, the learners' own language was very much excluded from the classroom. I remember my director of studies even went to the extent of suggesting that each student caught speaking Spanish pay a 'duro' (then five pesetas) to the teacher! Luckily, attitudes to own language use have changed a great deal since then. The updated Common European Framework of Reference (CEFR) now includes 'can-do' statements on translating from one language to another and mediating between languages. Plurilingual competence, central to the CEFR, also reflects the fact that classrooms today include not only students of very diverse language backgrounds but with very diverse linguistic goals.

The use of the students' own language is an important way of respecting their cultural identity and contributes to improved cognitive and linguistic development. Apart from being unrealistic and time-wasting in many contexts, an English-only approach can suggest to students that English is superior to their first or home language as it belongs to a dominant culture (see 5). The careful use of the learners' own language can then be seen as a way of providing them with reassurance and support in their learning.

Kerr (2019) has divided the way teachers use L1 in class into two main areas: the core and the social function. The core is related to the teaching of the language itself, for example, the explanation or checking the understanding of a grammar structure, while the social is related to classroom management, for example, building rapport, maintaining discipline, giving instructions and dealing with administrative issues. As regards inclusive practice, the social function is all important. As Kerr (2019, p. 19) says: 'Some tolerance of L1 may be a necessary condition in creating a safe speaking environment in which learners feel able to explore the limits of their language competence' (see **C**).

Practical ideas

For the students' own language to be used effectively in class, it is important that students understand when their L1 is allowed and when they are expected to use English only. Teachers can tell a class the 'language rules' (this can be included in the class contract) or this can be signalled in some way (see **7, 16**). You could use a pair of different flags to make this apparent to the students. Here are some practical ideas adapted from Kerr (2019) for using the L1 in its social function:

- **'Sandwiching':** For example, when giving instructions, you start in English, but if a particular item or structure proves problematic for the students, after saying it in English, give the equivalent translation in the L1 and finally say it again in English. That would work something like this in Spanish: 'Now, everybody get into groups of three, *formad grupos de tres,* get into groups of three and check your answers.' If items or structures are repeatedly 'sandwiched' in this way, students should eventually acquire them. You can display these kinds of instructional chunks of language around the classroom on cards or mini-posters so that students have a visual representation of them and they can be referenced easily.
- **Own language moments:** It is unrealistic to expect students who have trouble concentrating for long periods (e.g. some **neurodiverse** students) to use English throughout the lesson. To alleviate the pressure of using English, you can establish certain moments in class when students are allowed to use their own language. This can be particularly useful when the cognitive challenge is raised, for example, when students have to prepare for extended speaking tasks, give peer feedback or reflect on their own performance. Self-evaluation moments can help with students' motivation and self-esteem and if this can be done in their own language, it may signify more to them.

- **Cognates:** Many languages include words which are identical or similar to those in English. You can show a word like *banana* and ask students to say whether it is similar or different in their L1. Are the differences in spelling or pronunciation or both? It may be the case that some students are able to speak more than one language in which case you can get them to tell the class how the same word is expressed in their other languages. This is a technique that embraces translanguaging – the use of all of one's linguistic repertoire to communicate. Drawing on students' plurilingual resources is a way of helping them learn from their peers and feel included (see **13**).
- **Plurilingual approaches and materials:** For learners, seeing plurilingualism in their learning materials or methodology helps them to see that their own cultures and languages not only can be included in class but also have intrinsic value for others. There are many tasks that can involve students switching from one language to another. For example, students can read, watch or listen to a text and then summarize or paraphrase it in their own language or vice versa. They can research for English presentations by accessing texts in their L1 and they can unpack grammar explanations by contrasting English structures with their own language.

Another good way to exploit students' linguistic repertoire is to use their other languages to activate schemata or brainstorm ideas. For example, before doing a task we may want to gauge what the students already know about the topic by making cultural and linguistic comparisons. For example, you could ask, 'Does such a concept exist in your culture? Do you have an equivalent expression for X?'

Another good idea is to incorporate literary texts which include more than one language and then get the students to write short poems which contain an additional language that they may speak at home or are learning. You can also include video clips which feature a variety of voices and languages (Goldstein, 2023). Likewise, Mercer and Puchta (2023, p. 106) suggest working on poems, song lyrics, stories, 'focusing on the target language but using other languages as a bridge or even integral part of the creative text.' Examples of teenage students' work in multiple languages can be found here: https://www.creativeml.ox.ac.uk/blog/exploring-multilingualism/celebrating-linguistic-diversity-through-multilingual-poetry/index.html.

The amount of L1 used in class of course depends on your teaching context and your own knowledge and familiarity of the home language and culture. If you share that knowledge, then clearly you can exploit it a great deal. In plurilingual contexts where students do not share a community language, students' languages can still be used but in different ways. For example, a student can choose to present a text in their own language but make it accessible to all by using English to explain its meaning.

Council of Europe (2018) *Common European Framework of Reference for Languages: Learning, Teaching, Assessment Companion Volume with New Descriptors.* Strasbourg: Council of Europe. https://rm.coe.int/cefr-companion-volume-with-newdescriptors-2018/1680787989

Goldstein, B. (2023) Multilingualism in Language teaching: https://digitallearningassociates.com/whats-new/2023/2/10/multilingualism-in-language-learning

Kerr, P. (2019) The use of L1 in English language teaching. Part of the Cambridge Papers in ELT series. [pdf]: Cambridge University Press & Assessment. https://languageresearch.cambridge.org/images/CambridgePapersInELT_UseOfL1_2019_ONLINE.pdf

Mercer, S. and Puchta, H. (2023) *101 Psychological Tips.* Cambridge University Press & Assessment.

We like to believe that we make rational decisions about others in a reasonable way, but inevitably unconscious or implicit biases can permeate our way of thinking.

Essentially, such **biases** are attitudes or beliefs we are not aware of and affect how we think about those who are different from us. From these beliefs, automatic stereotypes and prejudices emerge and these influence how we perceive and interact with others.

Importantly, in an educational context, this can mean a teacher developing low or high expectations of a group or a student based on their own background and personal experience. For example, if you find yourself saying things like: 'Students from this part of town are worse at X than these others' or 'I like those students who volunteer to speak in class,' then you will be unconsciously excluding other students.

The Pygmalion effect

The impact that high or low expectations can have on performance is called *the Pygmalion effect*. For example, if you have high expectations of a class, it is more likely that the class will work harder to fulfill these expectations and, vice versa, if you have low expectations.

Imagine this other scenario: you have a new student in class, you know that their sibling showed little interest in learning English and was disruptive in class. You subsequently expect the new student to behave in the same way and treat them similarly (see **3**). If they are then disruptive in class, you may notice it more or tell them off more strongly than you would others. The student thus feels unfairly treated, becomes less motivated, and starts to lose interest as their sibling did. The scenario becomes 'a self-fulfilled prophecy' but, throughout this whole process, the teacher may be unaware of this unfair treatment.

To encourage an inclusive classroom environment, we need to fight against this kind of unconscious bias and give all our students the same opportunities to learn. How can we do this?

Practise self-reflection

Firstly, we have to be aware that we are not immune from these implicit biases and the stereotypical thinking around which they are based (see **22**). It can be uncomfortable to stop and recognize our own biases, but it is the main way that we can minimize their impact. Take some time to reflect on how these biases, as well as your position of privilege, may influence your interactions with students and the content of your classes (see **5**). You can take an Implicit Bias test (https://implicit. harvard.edu/implicit/takeatest.html) which measures how you might be impacted by bias. However, you should bear in mind the limitations of such tests as they are generally not accurate at detecting bias from a one-off use. In addition, simply taking such a test or reflecting on its results is not sufficient to effect real change. This is best achieved through constant reflection and acknowledgement of when bias is occurring, where it is coming from and most importantly, how it can be mitigated. For example, can you relate to any of these contexts?

1   You hear certain professions mentioned and visualize a male or a female for each (e.g. a nurse, engineer, beautician or CEO).
2   A taxi driver in your hometown looks different or has a strong accent, you ask, 'Where are you from?', when it is quite possible that they were born in the same country as you.

In both cases, we are making judgements about an individual based on a stereotype about the group to which we feel that person belongs. There may be no real harm in categorizing people in these ways. Problems emerge when we act *unfairly* based on those assumptions and/or cause a person harm, for example, if we discipline a student for arriving late without being sensitive to external factors (e.g. family matters) which could have influenced their lateness.

Avoid microaggressions

Microaggressions are comments or actions which undermine a person's identity by playing into biases. Some may be unintentional and even appear well-meaning. For example, the phrase 'all lives matter' (something you may hear politicians say) could be read at first as a term celebrating the worth of all humanity. However, it is commonly used in opposition to the Black Lives Matter (BLM) movement and there lies the confusion. The motto BLM was not intended to mean that other lives do not matter, it refers to the fact that Black people, who face **racism** and **discrimination**, have a voice that must be heard. 'All lives matter' only undermines that message and has thus become a well-disguised racist term.

Microaggressions are often levelled at **disabled** people. For example, it is common for people to adopt a patronizing tone or speak in an excessively slow or simple manner to a person with a **disability**. You may hear phrases like, 'It's so inspiring to see you doing this, considering your disability,' which may seem inoffensive or even compassionate, but only reinforces the stereotype of disabled people as helpless and in need of admiration (see **22**). The comment puts the disability before the person. Other examples betray a misunderstanding of a certain disability. For example, you may have heard people say, 'I'm not autistic, but I'm on the spectrum,' implying that they may share some behavioural traits with autistic people but at a low or barely noticeable level. Apart from being patronizing, this shows a lack of understanding of the terms *autism* and *spectrum* which should not be seen as a continuum from high- to low-performing individuals.

In a classroom setting, mispronouncing a student's name can be a microaggression which undermines their identity (see **5**). By choosing not to ask for correct pronunciation, you are saying that the student is different and it is not worth your getting their name right. Always ask for the correct pronunciation of names and record this if necessary so you can practise it.

As with all examples of unconscious bias, if you hear a microaggression, intervene politely by pointing out the effect of the action or comment on the person or community concerned.

Anecdote: Student bias

I worked for many years teaching English to teenagers in Hong Kong. My students largely came from upper-middle class backgrounds and had adopted English names. However, I remember once calling the register on the first day of class and a student made it clear to me that he did not have an English name, nor did he want one. Other students laughed at him, insinuating that this student was uncultured and belonged to an inferior social class. Looking back, I now see that this student's determination to retain his original name could have been to do with his need to retain his cultural identity rather than assume an Anglicized nickname which meant nothing to him. However, at that time, I remember having to resist adopting the biased opinion of his classmates. Now, looking back at this episode I see the whole issue of choosing Anglicized names as a past practice that may not be appropriate in an inclusive classroom. As McHenry (2023, p. 131) says: 'Acknowledging that students have the right to have their real names in the classroom is a crucial aspect of anti-racist pedagogy … it's up to teachers to make sure that the names we learn are the names the students want to be called.'

McHenry, T. (2023) 'No one can say it anyway: Personal names in the classroom' in Friedrich, P. (Ed.) *The Anti-Racism Linguist*, Multilingual Matters.

Using digital technology

Digital technology has brought huge benefits to neurodiverse students and those with disabilities. However, we need to maintain a critical eye with regard to its role in inclusive practice, in particular with respect to generative AI.

The Open University, the largest provider of higher education for people with disabilities in Europe, increased its percentage of students with a **disability** from three percent in 2011 to 18 percent in 2020 (UNESCO GEMR, 2023) thanks to the expansion of online formats and virtual learning environments. It is clear, therefore, that technology can help overcome many barriers faced by such students – providing multiple ways of representing information, offering personalized choices and, as a consequence, increasing engagement and motivation.

From assistive tools to digital devices

We have moved away from the days of assistive tools designed specifically for students with certain needs. Nowadays, an increasing number of platforms and devices, including smartphones, computers and tablets, boast embedded accessibility and personalization features, such as built-in screen readers, voice control, word prediction and customizable font sizes. These features make content more accessible to students with visual impairments or other reading difficulties. Importantly, they also have text-to-speech capability to provide support, particularly for dyslexic learners.

Likewise, for deaf students or those with partial hearing, speech-to-text software is also available on many devices, particularly tablets. This transcribes audio and video content to produce closed captions (or subtitles). Sound settings can also be adjusted to include a mono option (rather than standard stereo) and hearing aids can connect to many devices via Bluetooth. This can also be done live – even standard tools such as Google Meet and Zoom offer closed captioning.

There are also a number of tools related to readability. Many are simply extension links which are included within browsers such as Chrome. These include magnifiers, line height adjusters, colour overlays and so on which are particularly helpful for dyslexic students.

Tactile screens can be adjusted for students with dyspraxia so that a tapping rather than a swiping movement is made possible, thus making control easier. Screens can also be locked into position so that movement is reduced. For students with motor disabilities, tablets can provide a great sense of independence and control. Adaptations to trackballs, mice, switches and alternate keyboards can all facilitate learning and engagement for learners with physical disabilities.

Let us now look at two of the above areas in more detail:

Text to speech: One important growth area is the use of immersive readers which are sophisticated text-to-speech apps generated by AI. You can select any online text, and the reader will play it back to you as audio and allow you to personalize the content (e.g. altering the speed and **gender** of the voice reading the text). As for the text itself, you can colour different parts of speech or add labels to identify them, break words down into different syllables and translate items or the whole text into your language of choice. These readers also come with a picture dictionary and a pronunciation feature for lexical items. They also provide different colour backgrounds, font type and size, and a line focus that allows you to read one, three or five lines at a time. Some immersive readers also include a reading coach feature which allows you to record yourself reading the text. The coach will identify the words which proved the most challenging and suggest corrections. Others include an 'audio capture' capability which allows you to save the audio as an MP3 file.

Speech to text: In terms of speech-to-text software options, on a Google doc, simply talk into the mic icon and this will convert your voice into a text. Add emphasis and it will make the text go bold, say 'full stop', 'new line', etc. and the punctuation will also appear correctly in the finished text. Even with connected speech, voice recognition tools like these are relatively accurate and, of course, will improve in the future.

Such options exist in a number of familiar programs, such as Google Slides, which allow you to supplement your speech with closed captions (subtitles). Students can, of course, do this themselves. As they are talking about the slides, if they see an unintended word come up, they know they have made a pronunciation error. Such tools thus aid student's independent learning.

Even though these apps are readily available these days, students may not be aware that they have them and teachers may need training on how they can make the most of them. A simple tutorial in Microsoft Office will allow teachers to see how features such as Immersive Reader, Dictate, and Subtitles can be used for classes and class preparation.

Obviously assistive technologies, apps and digital tools become outdated and new ones appear all the time. For more information, I recommend Eric Curts' updated list at bit.ly/curts-support which focuses on Google Tools to Support All Learners and Understood www. understood.org which provides an enormous amount of resources for those with learning and thinking differences.

AI tools and bias

One thing to bear in mind when using such software and other AI-driven tools is the inherent **biases** within them. The majority of content in English used by the large language models that feed AI comes from the USA, so it goes without saying that such content will be slanted towards a Western worldview and its corresponding values. Its output, therefore, may well be inaccurate and lack the presence of diverse or **marginalized** voices, including languages other than English, thus potentially increasing digital inequality. Such bias also applies to AI detection tools (those used for identifying plagiarism in students' work) which have been found to place certain groups at a disadvantage, such as non-native English speakers or neurodivergent students, as well as those who may use simpler language or sentence structures.

AI's 'alignment problems' can prove an issue because they may not be immediately obvious to students. Indeed, it may be necessary to point out that AI chatbots are not neutral but trained on vast quantities of data created by humans. As such, they reflect our prejudices and biases. However, it is likely that some errors that AI-driven tools make will gradually be ironed out once their models get trained on a wider range of different written texts. The same will apply to audio and video input.

Despite these criticisms of bias and inaccuracy, there are, of course, positive uses of Gen AI when it comes to inclusive practice. For example, chatbots can be used to check texts for inclusive language and identify the very same biases that it produces! Students can also compare the output of different chatbots to identify their strengths and weaknesses and the types of biases reflected in each. Importantly, any attempts students make to humanize or personalize AI-produced output is likely to make it more inclusive. For example, if a chatbot produces stereotypical images of people from the students' country, more inclusive alternatives can be suggested by using carefully worded prompts.

Conclusion: The role of technology

The fact that accessible technology devices and generative AI are replacing traditional assistive tools is an important step forward. However, challenges for learners with disabilities remain in many parts of the world, where restricted access to education technology and connectivity is a major concern, as it is for all learners lacking in resources (see **17**). Technology has the power to level the playing field but it also risks widening the gap – the **digital divide** – between those with existing access to technology and those without. Other challenges include the risks inherent in the increasing digitalization of our societies, including the implications for students' well-being. Some examples include cyberbullying and hate speech.

For this and other reasons, technology should be used with caution. This point is made in the UNESCO (2023, p. 44) document *Technology in education: a tool on whose terms?* 'The most effective interventions are those that put learners' interests as the focal point and support human interaction, making use of adequate in-person support, extensive teacher training and appropriate technology for the specific context. The best learning systems never rely on technology alone.'

UNESCO Global Education Monitoring Report (2023) *Technology in education should comply with global accessibility standards* https://world-education-blog.org/2023/09/26/technology-in-education-should-comply-with-global-accessibility-standards/

UNESCO (2023) *Technology in education: a tool on whose terms?* https://www.unesco.org/gem-report/en/technology. https://doi.org/10.54676/UZQV8501

C: The learning environment

Inclusive practice is about creating the right atmosphere for learning and building a sense of trust and community, be that in the face-to-face or online classroom. Students will feel more themselves, and be more engaged if this **safe space** is created.

13 **Encouraging peer learning**

Peer learning means students learn with and from each other based on their particular strengths. This equitable interaction can foster empathy and mutual support, both of which are central to an inclusive class environment.

Benefits of peer learning

1 Research (Adams, 2018) suggests that when speaking with a language learner peer (rather than a more proficient speaker), learners speak more and for longer. With peers, students also experiment more with language, are less afraid to make mistakes and feel able to question each other's ideas more freely.

2 Peer learning allows students to get to know each other on a personal level and this can help break down **biases** based on difference (see **11**). By collaborating directly, students get to know each other as people and may be more able to discover their peers' strengths, rather than relying on pre-conceived ideas.

3 For learners with low levels of motivation, peer learning can have a positive effect on self-efficacy. Simply observing colleagues performing something well can give confidence to do the same. It is very much a case of 'If you can do it, I can too!'

4 Every student has their own stories to tell. Peer interaction can provide a platform for these diverse experiences, which may go unheard in teacher-student interaction or in a whole class setting as students may feel too intimidated to share them.

5 Learners get a chance to socialize and have conversations (Adams, 2018). This collaboration allows students to learn how to start or join a conversation, to take turns, change the subject, etc., which are all useful skills beyond the classroom. In this way, students learn to become part of a community of language learners, and this provides them with a sense of group belonging (see **30**).

Strategies for encouraging peer learning

However intuitively appealing peer learning is, some teachers may not be used to allowing students such freedom in class and some students may not see the benefit of learning from each other. Indeed, both may dismiss peer interaction as 'play', or as a poor substitute for chances to communicate with the teacher or other proficient speakers of the target language. So, here are some ideas for how peer learning can be applied in class successfully:

- Make peers accessible role models. Murphey and Murakami (1998, p. 18) suggest the following three steps:

  1 'Decide on (or discover within your group of students) the characteristics of good learners that you wish other students to emulate.
  2 Find (or produce) examples of these characteristics already among your students.
  3 Give these examples more exposure so that students can see, hear, or read about them (naturally model them).'

- Don't pair students based on language proficiency alone. Many teachers think of peer learning as simply pairing more advanced learners with those of a basic level or giving students with specific needs an education assistant. While for some tasks this might be desirable, it is also beneficial to consider students' content knowledge. For example, if you know that a particular student has lots of ideas about a particular topic or certain experience of it, pair them with another who may know less but is a more fluent speaker. In this way, both students benefit from the interaction in different ways.
- Share learning histories or action logs with your class. These do not need to be stories from students in your class but rather written or recorded accounts of other learners' experiences (e.g. the challenges, strategies and choices they face). These can then be compared with your students' experiences. Students can create their own histories or action logs after seeing the work of their peers.
- Consider working with peer dialogues. These can be recorded and viewed (or listened to) by other learners in a peer group.

They provide exposure to natural variations in pronunciation, reflecting the diverse way English is used in the world – highlighting examples of conversation that may not be perfect but are successful and effective in terms of communication. This can help learners understand that in order to communicate successfully, their speech does not have to be entirely free from errors.

- Model interactional skills. Although you have convinced students of the benefits of peer learning and interaction, you may need to model certain phrases explicitly for students to try out. For example:

Requesting clarification: *What does X mean?*
Providing feedback: *I think we say it like …*
Requesting confirmation: *Do you mean …?*
Requesting input: *What do you think of …? What did you put for …?*
Narrowing focus: *I don't understand this word; Instead, let's look at …*

Example: Peer role models in *Evolve*

I worked on an adult coursebook series for Cambridge University Press & Assessment called *Evolve* (2018). One of its most interesting features is the inclusion of a series of student contributors. Each level has speakers from different countries and backgrounds, and they are more or less the same level as the students using the course. Students watch short videos of these contributors on their phones via QR codes embedded in the unit contents. The videos were made by the peers themselves on their mobile phones and in their homes. This also encourages students to empathize with them. The contributors do the same tasks as the students in class, so their monologues act as useful scaffolding. They are essentially peer role models offering the students in class the chance to watch people 'like them' (with their accents and errors) as opposed to the 'perfect' English native speaker role model (see **10, 14**).

The focus here is on international intelligibility and effective communication, not striving for an inaccessible model. In this way, variations in students' different Englishes (e.g. pronunciation) are seen as enriching and empowering. By empathizing with the contributors, students see themselves within the material and feel included. The closeness of the peer is the real asset here as it is both motivating and empathic for students to see people like them within their language learning materials (see **14**). They can better identify learning goals and see that they are achievable. Watching these peers also prepares them for the real English speaking world where variability is the norm.

Adams, R. (2018) Enhancing student interaction in the language classroom: Part of the Cambridge Papers in ELT series. [pdf] Cambridge University Press & Assessment.

Clandfield, L., Goldstein, B., Hendra, L., Ibbotson, M., O'Dell, K., Jones, C. and Kerr, P. *Evolve* (2018) Cambridge University Press & Assessment.

Murphey, T. and Murakami, K. (1998) 'Teacher facilitated near peer role modelling for awareness raising within the Zone of Proximal Development', *Academia* 65, 1–29.

14   Developing empathy

Demonstrating empathy in class helps build connections and develops an environment of trust and cooperation. It is impossible to create an inclusive environment without developing a sense of empathy.

In a survey (Mercer and Kostoulas, 2018, p. 164) based on interviews with secondary level language teachers, empathy was found to be the most notable element in a positive student-teacher relationship: 'All of the teachers spoke of trying to get on the kids' wavelength ... they displayed qualities of empathy in how they spoke about their pupils, seeking to understand their behaviour rather than judging them.' This research shows how good teachers strive to understand their learners' perspectives, care about their experiences and are sensitive to the language they use and behaviour they model. Now that we have established the importance of developing empathy, here are some ideas to help you do this.

Activities

1   Set up role plays to allow students to imagine another person's reality. For those who don't like talking about themselves, using characters from a story as a first step can help students focus. Having done that, they can move on to more personal questions like, *Which person do you empathize with and why? Can you remember when you last felt the same way?* This step-by-step approach allows students to gradually open up.

2   Work with images or video (with sound off) in which two people are present, preferably in a situation which could trigger students' imaginations. Where possible, choose people from distinct groups that aren't represented in your class, alongside others. First, ask students to write speech bubbles for the characters, then add thought bubbles to show what they are imagining. Students can then act out their dialogue. If using a video, you can show the scene with

sound on and compare it to the dialogue created by the students. As a follow-up writing task, students could reflect further on this particular scene and write out the thoughts and feelings from one of the people's perspectives.

3   Choose an example from popular culture which features people with diverse identities. For example, the Netflix series 'Sex Education' represents a school community with a number of marginalized students: neurodivergent, working class, gay, trans, **Black**, physically **disabled** and deaf. Indeed, though a comedy, the series seriously examines how schools become inclusive institutions and the lessons learned along the way. It anaylses important topics from becoming empowered and understanding your own worth to bullying and depression, among others.

Classroom management

When you can, practise active listening and open communication with your students, making eye contact, nodding and providing verbal and non-verbal cues to show you are engaged (see **9**). Model empathy and respect especially when students show low self-esteem. For example, if a student seems withdrawn or unwilling to work with others, ask them to take on an observer's role and report back what they saw when the task is over. Likewise, if a student is avoiding an activity because it is too demanding, allow them to choose an easier one (see **8**). In any case, you may need to make time to speak to the student in question. When doing so, ensure the language you use is supportive and non-judgmental (e.g. *You don't seem yourself, is there something upsetting you or that you want to talk about?*).

Mercer and Puchta (2023, p. 85) suggest that it is often 'better to delay a reaction to what a student says … We often react to the verbal message and give advice to a student, while ignoring the emotional meta-message. It is the answer to the *second* question that can help us show empathy, by saying, for example: 'You must be quite (*annoyed*) about what happened, / I can imagine that this makes you feel (*excited*).' Sometimes being listened to and feeling understood may be all that is needed at that moment.

Organize *appreciation circles* where students can share something positive they saw another student doing. This could be a skill or positive quality they observed. Appreciation circles work equally well with children and adults and could become a regular feature of your class time. You can repeat the activity to rotate through all class members. Alternatively, for younger children, it might be easier to create an appreciation box in which students can post their written positive statements about each other. These could then be shared and the statements kept by each student. Names can also be drawn out of a hat to prevent a situation where some students are not 'appreciated' by others, as this may only increase their sense of exclusion.

Keep a journal to record instances of yourself, a student or a colleague being empathic. Note these down in as much detail as possible as they may act as good models in the future.

'Caring for' and 'caring with'

Hunter (2023, p. 2), quoting Dávila and Linares (2020), makes an interesting distinction between 'caring for' and 'caring with' students (see **30**). The former is one that most people associate with teaching and involves developing a sense of empathy and trust. While 'caring with', she argues, is about 'developing strong interpersonal relationships with students and their families, learning about and from them, respecting and affirming their language and culture, and building on these to support learning.'

The following anecdote from Juan Lopes, a Brazilian teacher (sent by personal correspondence in video format), I think shows a teacher both 'caring for' and 'caring with' their students. It dates from the time of the COVID pandemic and highlights a particular moment that showed the great trust that he shared with the group:

I had the feeling that the lesson wasn't going anywhere ... because of the trauma that we were going through together so I just decided to open up about the losses I'd had, so did students and we had this liberating moment when we could just talk about our feelings.

Juan told me he believed the online teaching environment (see **17**) made it strangely easier for him to open up to his students. He is, of course, referring to a specific context with adult students and you may not feel comfortable showing that kind of vulnerability, but his testimony shows how empathic any language classroom can be at a moment of real need.

It is important to highlight here Juan's ability to perceive the feelings of the students (particularly in a virtual environment) and use that understanding to guide his actions. It is a great example of listening to feelings *behind* a person's words. But I think the anecdote also shows that being empathic should go beyond the idea of stepping into someone else's shoes: it should give students an appreciation as to why it is important for them to care.

Hunter, A. (2023) 'Trouble and care in the English language classroom' in Hunter, A. (Ed.) *Diversity and English Language Education: Supporting learners through Research and Practice*. Routledge.

Mercer, S. and Kostoulas, A. (Eds.) (2018) *Language Teacher Psychology*. Multilingual Matters.

Mercer, S. and Puchta, H. (2023) *101 Psychological Tips*. Cambridge University Press & Assessment.

Handling conflict and prejudice

> However well-intentioned the content of your classes
> might be and however careful you are with classroom
> management, there will be moments when students don't
> collaborate or even become confrontational.

In some contexts, these are known as *hot moments* – when a student
comes out with a harmful or offensive comment against individuals
or groups usually with **marginalized** identities. These moments can be
difficult to anticipate and can create conflict – threatening to interrupt
the class. It is important, therefore, to prepare yourself with strategies
should these moments arise.

Calling in and calling out

Calling in and *calling out* have become popular concepts for dealing
with such moments but, in many ways, they represent opposite
strategies. Calling in is about taking a rational perspective to the
moment and talking calmly to the person who made the comment.
If you call in, you ask questions to learn more about the student and
where this comment came from. Calling in is not about confronting the
student but turning the moment into a learning opportunity. It is also
a way of fostering awareness and providing students with alternative
perspectives. When calling in, try to avoid leading questions, *Yes/No*
questions and questions with only one answer. Structure questions to
encourage student interaction and don't be afraid of silence – waiting
for an answer indicates that you want a thoughtful response.

Five possible calling in responses:

- *Hey, that's a strong word. What do you mean by that / X?*
- *Stop and think for a moment. What did you really mean to say
  there?*
- *Right, where did you hear that? What impact do you think it could
  have on …?*

- *OK … right. But how might someone else see this differently?*
- *Let's talk about what you just said. What assumptions are you making here about …?*

Calling out is a much more direct approach. When you call out, you need to stop the comment in its tracks before the moment can get out of hand and lead to more harm. Call out when you need to let the student know that the comment is unacceptable. Try this when attempts at calling in have not worked and/or the offensive comments are repeated.

Five possible calling out responses:

- *Hey, I need to stop you right there! I don't want to hear that in this class.*
- *Wait, that is not the right thing to say. It does not represent our class's values at all.*
- *Why is that so funny? Can you tell me because it's not at all funny to me?*
- *Hey, wait a moment. You have to realize how harmful that comment is to X.*
- *It sounded like you said X. You have to understand that that is not appropriate.*

So, for example, imagine you are in class when a teenage student says (referring to a cultural group), 'Urrgh, those people eat dogs,' during an activity about food and festivals. The calling-out strategy would be saying something very direct like: *What did you say? That is racist! We don't say that in our classroom. Stop.* On the other hand, calling in could involve a conversation, like this one taken from the webinar 'How do you respond to insensitive language in the classroom?' by Verónica Higareda (you would need to adapt the language for an adult learner):

Teacher: Ah, really? Is that true? How do you know that?

Student: I don't know. I just heard it.

Teacher: Ah, careful then. We mustn't spread rumours. It's not kind. And, in this classroom we are kind.

Student: But it's weird and disgusting. They are pets!

Teacher: Can you think of some 'weird' or 'disgusting' food we eat here [Spain]. Aren't rabbits pets?

Other student(s): Snails, blood pudding, peas!

Notice that the teacher elicits responses from other students to back up the calling-in approach.

Calling in can often be the best strategy because the comment may be a result of cultural differences and language barriers. It might just be a case of paraphrasing the comment (e.g. saying *low-income* rather than *poor*). If so, it is a good idea to give students multiple chances to self-correct. Finally, recognize the role of your own interpretation and approach the comment with curiosity and not just rejection, especially if the comment is at all ambiguous.

Effect on the student

The effect on the student of being called in or called out is radically different, especially for children. If called out, the child realizes that they have said something wrong, harmful or offensive and feels ashamed of it in front of others. As a result, they will most likely become defensive. However, the student is not told why or given the chance to rectify their comment.

On the other hand, if called in, the student is made to realize the impact of the comment on others. Very often, students come out with stereotypical comments like the above (e.g. 'All X people are …'). If that is the case, it is relatively easy to retort using the student's nationality: *OK, so, how would you feel if someone said that all X people are Y?* This encourages reflection and empathy and makes students realize that *essentialist* readings are unacceptable (see **22**).

Calling in or calling out?

Hot moments are referred to as such because they happen in the heat of the moment, so it is a good idea to give yourself a bit of time before responding one way or the other and remain calm. While you pause, think about when it is best to deal with the comment. Does it have to be addressed immediately, or can it be returned to later more calmly? Consider your body language: a brief pause or a surprised look may be enough in the moment to make the student realize there is something wrong. There may also be topics which 'activate' you more than others.

Likewise, if you plan to discuss a sensitive topic, you should warn students beforehand. If the material you use or the methodology you adopt is more **disruptive** (see **22**), then it is more likely that there will be hot moments as certain topics will come to the fore that do not normally appear. Before taking a disruptive approach, make sure that you are confident that these hot moments can be avoided: try to anticipate your students' responses.

I recently took a course and was asked the following questions before the course started in a private and confidential online exchange with the teacher:

1   Are there any topics, words or language that are triggering for you that you would prefer to avoid discussing?
2   Is there anything about the course that you feel apprehensive about?
3   Do you have any additional needs that you would like to make me aware of?

This kind of preparation will help you ascertain if there are topics which could prove particularly problematic. At the same time, you should let students know that if they feel offended by anything in particular then they should be able to say so in class, even though this might make them appear overly sensitive. Finally, consider the classroom context: some students prefer to discuss inclusive topics online rather than in a face-to-face environment, particularly in discussion forums.

Higareda, V. Webinar: 'How do you respond to insensitive language in the classroom?' (British Council – Breaking Down Barriers Mini-Series) https://youtu.be/QquJzPClQuk?si =bADhwelbXuK739hZ&t=2315 From 38.35 (accessed 6 December 2024)

In order to build a sense of community and respect in class, certain norms and values may need to be established explicitly. Here, we look at practical ways that a sense of community can be developed in class.

Modelling respect

One of the most important ways teachers can support building community in an inclusive classroom is by modelling respect. This is crucial as however much our students claim that they are free of **bias** and prejudice, the presence of students who are 'different' from the **norm** may lead many to think their education is being diminished in some way. Respect is fundamentally about getting students to value the contribution made by everybody in class, however different each person's outlook and lived experience may be.

From the teacher's point of view, modelling respect is about good manners and sensitive practice, for example, using learners' names correctly (see **9, 10**), including interventions for certain students (see **7**) and allowing for student choice (see **8**). As the class is a community, many of the rules involving respect should actually be the same for teachers and students alike. Indeed, a very simple way to build community is to refer to your relationship with your students as 'we' and 'us', rather than 'me' and 'you'. These references can be made clear both in classroom language and in a class contract based on shared values.

Class contracts

Class contracts can work for all age groups but, of course, their rules or norms will be quite different in nature. With younger learners, there will be questions of discipline and protocol (e.g. punctuality) that won't be needed with adults or at least not to the same extent. I have suggested five different norms below as a starting point for each age bracket, but you might well need to modify these for your specific context and learner profiles.

Another option is to get the students to think of their own rules first (in their own language if need be) and work from there. This is best done by establishing a fixed number of norms which students plan in pairs or small groups, and which can then be modified whilst working with another group. In the end, there should be a whole class consensus on the top norms to include which you, of course, should approve. Once you have established the content of the contract, don't forget to sign it along with your class!

Some students will have lots of ideas, but others might need prompting, so you could ask questions to set them off such as: *What things would you like your classmates to do more / less of? Why?* or *What would you like to learn more / less of? Why?* It is a good idea to combine language learning norms with behavioural ones, even for younger students.

The important thing to remember about class contracts is that they are not intended to prevent inappropriate behaviour and comments (see **15**); these will most likely occur in your class in any case. Instead, think of the contract as a way to involve your class in establishing norms that will support an inclusive learning environment. Consistently enforcing your contract together with your students is a great way to establish that environment successfully.

A Adult learners

- Show respect for other students, use their preferred names and pronouns.
- Listen carefully to other people's opinions and do not interrupt.
- Try not to jump to conclusions or make assumptions, be curious and ask questions.
- Respect the point a student makes even if you disagree. When showing disagreement, criticize the idea not the person.
- Keep an open mind with the expectation of learning something new.

B Teenage learners

- Be kind and caring toward others.
- Be respectful listeners.

- Share your ideas.
- Arrive at class on time.
- Use mobile phones only when the teacher tells you.

C Young learners

- Be kind.
- Hand in your homework on time.
- Try your best.
- Listen to others.
- Speak in English when you can.

Finally, remember that class contracts are fluid documents and should be revisited where necessary. For example, revisions might be needed before using more disruptive materials (see **22**), dealing with a particularly challenging topic (see **15**), or if students feel that they or members of the class are not adhering to any of the norms on a regular basis. Finally, class contracts should refer to both student and teacher behaviour: a joint discussion about what to include and why will be crucial to the contract's success and workability.

Core values

Another way of building a community is to examine different values and get the class to rank them in order of importance. By the end of the activity, students should have a set of core values that define their particular classroom community. Just as with the contract, the idea is for students to reflect in pairs or small groups first and then to come to a consensus about which values need prioritizing.

Below is an example of ten different values to be ranked by teens/adult students. These have been adapted from the University of Michigan's Equitable Teaching website:

Tolerance: Being respectful of others
Creativity: Finding new ways of doing things
Belonging: Being connected to and liked by others
Teamwork: Cooperating with others towards a common goal
Courage: Standing up for yourself, overcoming fears
Community: Building common goals and values
Tradition: Respecting the ways things have always been done

Competition: Winning, outdoing others
Diplomacy: Finding common ground and resolving conflict with people
Excellence: Striving for perfection

As with the classroom contract, the idea is to keep updating the set. There may be values that do not currently appear and could be added subsequently.

For young learners, a values syllabus has become a feature of many classrooms but very often these values are simply placed on the wall or attached to stories and other learning materials in an artificial way. Rather than seeing it just as a feature of a coursebook unit, it is good to incorporate these values into your everyday inclusive practice. You can display the values on the wall, referring to them regularly and then get the students to illustrate them or brainstorm other words associated with them. Another idea is to team up with a partner school in another country to create an authentic intercultural exchange, using positive reinforcement (e.g. praising examples of the core values you want to promote in class).

University of Michigan Equitable Teaching. https://sites.lsa.umich.edu/inclusive-teaching/core-values/

17

Working in online classrooms

> Many of us are now used to online classrooms yet
> overlook barriers to learning that have emerged due to
> the digital divide. Here, we look at issues related to digital
> equity and best practice for teaching online.

More and more language classes are now taught online. However, these
learning environments vary enormously. You might find yourself in
an asynchronous space in which students work independently and/or
contribute to a group forum, or synchronously when students are in a
live class via a conferencing program such as Zoom.

However different these contexts are, teachers tend to have less
control over their students' experience in online classes than face-to-
face. We can't know, for example, how conducive the student's home
environment is for learning, how reliable the internet connection is
and so on. This is true for all students, but when teaching inclusively,
it is important to bear in mind the **digital divide** before online classes
begin. A good way to do this is to pose questions to raise awareness. In
common with many inclusive strategies, always consider these questions
as a starting point rather than an afterthought.

This list provides you with some ideas. Following each set of questions
are some notes to guide you if you find there are students encountering
barriers in these areas. If teaching younger children, present these
questions to their parents. However, bear in mind that some families
may not have appropriate technology and that these questions should
be confidential to avoid risk of embarrassment.

1 Questions to ask students before start of the course

Connectivity

- *Do you have access to an internet connection?*
- *If so, how stable/fast is it?*

- *Do you have access to your own digital device (mobile, laptop, tablet, computer) for attending classes? If you have to share, can you reserve a device in advance?*
- *Are there likely to be power cuts when accessing the class? If so, are these announced beforehand?*

Bear in mind that classes with live video and audio conferencing such as Zoom require higher bandwidth than asynchronous classes, as do working with collaborative documents such as Google Docs and group chat or messaging. Email, pre-recorded audio and video and discussion boards with text and images require far lower bandwidth and therefore may be more versatile tools depending on your context.

Remember that large files can also overload email or not reach their destination, so consider compressing images and other heavy documents (e.g. https://tinypng.com). Captions may be required for videos for a number of reasons, e.g. for students who are deaf or hard of hearing, but also for those working in quiet spaces or without headphones (e.g. https://www.veed.io/tools/add-subtitles) (see **13**).

Digital skills

As above, these questions should be asked confidentially and individually for reasons of sensitivity.

- Operational: *How confident are you using computer equipment and the internet?*
- Informational/Navigational: *How much experience have you had finding information online, evaluating and verifying it?*
- Social: *Are you able to communicate and socialize online easily?*
- Creative: *To what extent have you created and shared content online?*
- For all four skills, add: *Have you encountered any barriers doing this? If so, what have they been?*

Younger students now have a greater exposure to digital technologies, but we can't assume that they have the necessary digital skills to use them effectively. In particular, the concept of the *digital native* (the idea that young people pick up these skills whatever the context) can be a harmful one when thinking of inclusive practice as many **marginalized** groups may not have had the necessary access to technology to develop such skills. Similarly, if your younger students are tech-savvy, it doesn't mean that they are digitally wise. It is crucial to establish a code of conduct and AUP (acceptable use policy) with students – even better if negotiated with the students themselves – to guarantee students' safety online (see **12**).

Study environment

- *Are you able to work in a quiet space at home during class time? Are there any barriers to learning (noise, comfort, inability to talk)?*
- *If your home environment is not conducive to language learning, are there any alternative places you can go?*
- *Are people at home supportive of your studies, for example, are they willing to adjust their own habits or behaviour to allow you to study? Can they help with any of the above digital skills, e.g. accessing information online?*

In the case of younger students, the attitude and support of parents is vital for students to study successfully at home, as is parental mediation. The latter may take the form of suggestions on how to use the internet safely, control in blocking children's access to certain online content and warnings about online misinformation.

2 Best practice

Once you have answers to the above questions, it's important to be flexible enough to consider different options whilst teaching online. Here are some ideas as well as notes on best practice:

- **Offer student choice.** If students' internet is unreliable or digital devices are scarce, allow them to present their work in the format that they find easiest – audio, video, text, image, etc. (see **8**).

- **Be flexible.** For example, where possible, change deadlines from a fixed date to a window to avoid giving students extra stress. This will allow students to plan their time better. Other options include recording the lesson so students can catch up at a later date if they miss a class.

- **Vary delivery mode** when teaching synchronously to avoid distractions. Shift between breakout rooms, open-ended responses and chat (both to whole class and privately for feedback and instructions). Allow students to share screens and provide input. If appropriate, take a break away from the screen or set an activity which obliges students to get up and move around. Also exploit messaging apps (e.g. WhatsApp) which many students are able to access on their phones and may be the most reliable means of out-of-class communication.

- **Check-in early**. Where possible, start your live session a minute or two early. This will give everyone time to connect and check that everyone can use the key functions (e.g. chats, muting mic and activating cameras) and has done any pre-class tasks.

- **Plan for interruptions**, for example, if the connection is unreliable. Warn students of the protocol if there is a long interruption. For instance, establish the homework beforehand and ask students to prepare for it. Be flexible about break times to allow for distractions and interruptions.

- **Be proactive**. Setting tasks for students to engage with in advance reduces the pressure for everything to be covered in the live session. This also means students will be better prepared, particularly important if students' internet connections are poor that day or they have to miss a session.

- **Bear in mind the learning environment** when setting tasks. If students are in a noisy place, ask them to record video instead of doing a speaking task. If students are at home, ask them to take something from their space to share with others. 'Show and tell' is a great task in which students find a meaningful object and explain to their classmates why it is important to them. Also consider the devices the students are using to connect. For example, if using mobile phones don't set long reading texts.

- **Build in time** for questions and personalized feedback (via chat). This is much more important online than face-to-face to reduce misunderstandings. Audio and video feedback is better still but more time-consuming, particularly if done on an individual basis.

- **Establish certain rules.** Learning online can be isolating for some students, and they may retreat more by turning off their cameras. Other students are more active online than in the face-to-face class. Certain rules can help maximize communication and collaboration for all, for example, with reference to webcam use, mic muting, turn taking, asking questions, break-out rooms and chat functions. Improving the clarity of your visual communication with regard to text (e.g. readable font), graphics, layout and formatting is key in this respect.

- **Give instructions and learning outcomes.** This is even more important in online environments where students are prone to distraction and lose focus more easily. Having a space where instructions are always visible, for example, in the chat or at the top of the screen is one way to guarantee that students can always refer to them. Other options include asking students to take a screenshot of the instructions or asking students to repeat them, as you might do in any class. With regard to learning outcomes, make a slide of the lesson agenda outlining what students will be doing in class and why, and tick these off as you go. This can be particularly useful for students with reduced ability to recall and process information.

Case Study: The SCALED Project

Run by the University of Warsaw, the aim of the SCALED project is to create an online course preparing teachers for inclusive teaching, **universal design** for learning (see **7** and **24**) and increased accessibility in language education, especially with regard to **neurodiverse**, blind students or those with low vision. The course, based around ten modules, is open access and well worth taking.

Nijakowska, J., Tsagari, D. and Guz, E. (Eds.) (2023) *SCALED Course – Increasing accessibility in language education.* SCALED project. https://scaled.uw.edu.pl/output-2/

D: Materials: Inclusive representation

One of the most direct ways to embrace inclusive practice is to use inclusive materials. These can help develop empathy, challenge stereotypes and, importantly, provide students with contexts they recognize and the necessary language to describe themselves and their lives.

18

Analysing materials: Visual representation

There is greater diversity of representation in ELT materials these days but there is still a good deal of work to be done. Analysing materials according to inclusive criteria is a good way to start you on the path to adapting and/or writing your own.

One way to start an analysis is by creating a list of questions about the nature of the content. Here is a checklist to get you developing a critical eye. When you start out, it's a good idea to focus on a narrow area of analysis otherwise the task can become unwieldy. In this case, the questions focus on how people are represented visually. There is a lot here, so pick and choose the questions you find most relevant to your context and start with those.

Take a look at some sample pages of the materials that you are using at present and focus on the images of people. Make sure that you choose pages which are representative of the materials as a whole and show a number of different contexts, then reflect on the following questions:

Person/Identity

- What cultures and ethnicities are represented and how?
- What social class do the people belong to? How do you know?
- What age groups are represented?
- Do you see a range of body types?
- How about relationship types?
- Is there **gender** variety? If so, how much?
- Are any **marginalized** groups represented? If so, how are they portrayed?

- Is any identity type centred more than others? If so, what is the effect of that?
- Would you say there is a sufficient variety of identities represented?
- Do you feel that any identities are not represented? If so, how could they be better represented?

Activity/Attitude

- What are the people doing?
- Are roles differentiated and/or stereotyped according to gender? If so, how?
- Consider the same question for people of different social and ethnic groups.
- How would you describe the people's mood or attitude?
- Are they looking directly at the camera or not? Are they smiling? Why is this important?

Authenticity

- Are the people represented in a natural or real-world way? Why? Why not?
- Where do you think the images were sourced? How do you know? / How can you guess?

Equity

- Is the representation of these people a fair one? Does it suggest an inferior reality?
- Does it reflect an authentic everyday reality or an exoticized other one?

Effect on the viewer

- What part do you think these representations of people play in motivating your learners?
- Do you identify or empathize with them? Why? Why not?
- Do you think your students could see themselves in the representations? Why? Why not?

- Do you detect any **bias,** prejudice or stereotyping in these visual representations?
- If so, how is that manifested?

Role of the image

- Is the representation integral to an activity or merely decorative?
- If decorative, does it transmit any particular message?

The above questions focus on images but, of course, you can go through a similar analysis with any part of the material. For example, you could pose questions related to the audio component such as:

- Are there a variety of different Englishes and accents represented? If so, how many?
- Are the voices authentic sounding? Why? Why not? If not, give examples.
- Is there a range of international speakers and contexts? Which could be adapted?
- Does a prestige variety (e.g. one used by native speakers) dominate? If so, to what degree and effect?

Tokenism

After doing the above analysis, you may be surprised to discover your materials barely feature marginalized groups at all. However, even if there is a visible reference to a group, it's a good idea to be wary of **tokenism.** By tokenism, I mean that members of certain groups are visible, but their presence only serves to give an illusion of diversity. Tokenism is prevalent nowadays as publishers demand writers include a certain kind of diversity, particularly with regard to visual materials. Such apparent diversity allows the product to pass the 'flick through test' when a potential customer analyses the material in a superficial way to check for diversity of representation.

One way to check for this is to include a comparison of two editions of the same material, especially if there are a number of years between them. There you may well see how the representations have changed. For example, there may be a focus on an African community where a White Anglo-Saxon context had featured previously. But if people from this community are represented in a way which emphasizes their poverty, it may reinforce existing power relations, stereotypes and biases. This is an example of diversity but without inclusion (see **1**) – these people are visible, but they aren't given a voice. Likewise, if you find an image of a marginalized group, it is important to consider its function. If it is used symbolically or for decoration, it could be interpreted as a form of 'showcasing', reducing this person's identity to a one-off representation that is somehow exotic, special or different. This is, in fact, the antithesis of an inclusive approach. Indeed, in inclusive materials, it is often preferable *not* to draw attention to a marginalized group but rather present it alongside others in a way in which the group does not stand out (see usualized approach in **21**).

Takeaways

Finally, the best way to evaluate and analyse your materials is to ask the students' own opinions. If you wanted to do a formal analysis with your class, you could modify the above questionnaire according to your students' age and level, but an informal approach may work just as well. Simply by including questions of this type about materials can be a step in the right direction.

Whichever aspect you choose to analyse, it is worth remembering that materials and the representations within them shape the worldview of our students and can have a particularly strong effect on young learners. The stereotypes and biases present in materials, however subliminal, may hinder an otherwise inclusive methodology.

As Aow, Hollins and Whitehead (2023, p. 104) have commented: 'Representation has the power to create a 'new normal'. It is not simply about representation itself, but how this increased visibility creates new messages, stories and experiences for students that become a part of how they understand and interpret the world.'

Aow, A., Hollins, S. and Whitehead, S. (2023) *Becoming a Totally Inclusive School: A Guide for Teachers and School Leaders.* Routledge.

19

Analysing materials: Textual representation

As with visuals, we need to check that texts represent and give voice and agency to marginalized identities and avoid stereotyping and othering. Let's look at some examples where representation is found lacking in these respects.

Here we will be looking at particular texts and lessons. We will see that although certain texts foreground **marginalized** identities, that doesn't make them inclusive in anything other than a tokenistic and stereotypical way. In actual fact, they may be condescending and ultimately harmful to members of this community (see **22**).

Text example 1: Disability

One coursebook features a text about a blind teenage boy whose elder brother buys him a special football for his birthday; something which really surprises him. The ball has smaller balls inside it that make a noise when you kick or throw it. The problem with this context is that it is inauthentic and patronizing. First, it is unlikely that the blind boy wouldn't know of such a ball in the first place. Secondly, the focus here is on the blind boy's helplessness. He is 'saved' by his elder brother who knows what is best for him. It is the brother who has the power and agency. Finally, the ball is 'special' as it is seen from the able person's perspective. The text would be more inclusive if the blind boy asks his brother to give him the audible ball as a present, as it is something *he* wants. It would also help if this story was placed alongside that of another teenager talking about an entirely different present.

Questions to students

When analysing, it is good to look throughout the whole lesson to related follow-up questions based on the texts in question. For example, this question adapted from a coursebook for teens follows on from a reading text which practises the present perfect for life experiences. This is then followed by a focus on compound nouns related to the body and health (e.g. *wheelchair, painkiller,* etc.) To practise both the grammar and vocabulary at the end of the lesson, students then have to gap-fill a series of questions which they ask and answer in pairs. This is the first:

How often have you pushed someone in a _____ [wheelchair] because they couldn't walk?

In common with example 1 about the blind teenager, the question is written from an ableist point of view. It assumes that the reader themselves is not in a wheelchair! And it frames the person in the wheelchair by what they can *not* do (e.g. walk), thus **'othering'** their identity. An alternative question with the target vocabulary could be something like:

Are the spaces around desks in the classroom wide enough for students in _____ [wheelchairs] to get around easily?

Text example 2: Different cultures

Another coursebook text summarizes the idea of a TV programme which takes certain professionals from Canada and asks them to do their job in difficult conditions around the world. For example, a Toronto taxi driver tries out his job on the streets of Dhaka in Bangladesh, a firefighter goes to the Peruvian Andes and a nurse goes to the emergency department of a hospital in Maputo, Mozambique. The issue is that the original series (and hence the texts based on it) is centred on a dominant White and colonizing culture. The Canadian visitor is thrown into an 'uncivilized' society where working conditions are poor and challenging. The text thus emphasizes how hard it is for the visitor and does not feature voices from the different cultures at all. It assumes that the reader/student can identify with this worldview. A follow-up listening text focuses on a taxi driver from Dhaka, and chooses to represent the city in a one-dimensional and problematic way, emphasizing poverty and hardship.

As the text represents only stereotypical images of the developing world, it 'others' these cultures as places of suffering which require our pity. It is accompanied by images which emphasize this – crowds of masked people outside a hospital, traffic jams and forest fires. It is not hard to imagine students from these countries finding these representations harmful.

How could these texts be made more inclusive? One approach would be simply to turn this on its head and feature voices from the countries themselves: people talking about their experiences of showing these Canadian visitors their cultures. If these experiences could show some positive aspects of the said country, that would also be a step in the right direction. A more disruptive approach (see **21**) would be to actively critique the TV programme and its *raison d'etre*. This could be done in the text itself or in discussion questions to the students.

From this analysis, I hope it can be seen that it is not enough to consider texts in isolation, and that we also need to consider how they are contextualized and framed, and from what perspective they have been written.

We can see that a recurring problem in these examples is that people from certain communities (be they blind, in wheelchairs or from Bangladesh) are not given voice and agency and as such their representations are simplistic, stereotyped and potentially harmful.

As a general rule, if you come across any kind of text about a particular identity created by someone who does not belong to that group, then it is a good idea to analyse it with a critical eye. You could ask yourself these questions: *Who produced it? For what reason? Whose point of view does it adopt? Whose voices do we hear? How could it be made more inclusive?*

Even when there are quotations from the people concerned, it is worth considering the questions they were asked and if these provoke a certain or expected response from the interviewer's point of view. When choosing materials to use in class, it is often best to provide examples of people with marginalized identities alongside those who are not marginalized, so the former do not appear as special or in need of help (see **23**).

Imagine that you have some material that you want to use in class as the topic is of interest but, having analysed it, you realize that it is not representative, equitable or authentic. How do you go about such an adaptation? Let's look at some examples.

The first thing to do is to identify the degree to which the material needs adapting and what exactly needs changing – the texts, the images, the activities – bearing in mind the context in which it appears. How big a job is it? When adapting material to make it more inclusive, it is good to start with critical questions such as:

- Whose perspective is being centred by the text (i.e. what is the default position)?
- What unspoken messages are transmitted? How do you know?
- Is there another perspective or narrative which could be included instead or alongside the current one (see 6)?

In my experience, this default position can at times be difficult to spot because texts designed for language learning are often very factual in nature. This gives them a rather impersonal and flat quality, often because they are vehicles for comprehension-based tasks. For this reason, many need to be adapted to become not only more inclusive but also more engaging. Here are two different ways of adapting materials for adult level students, one of my own and another from a colleague.

Example 1: 'Hygge'

This text based on the subject of *Hygge* – the Danish concept of 'coziness', of relaxing and feeling at home – was accompanied by images of good-looking, White, middle-class people sitting in expensive homes. The concept itself was promoted uncritically as an ideal lifestyle choice so it was not difficult to uncover the material's unspoken messages nor whose perspective was being centred. The text and images set up

Denmark (the seventh richest country in the world) as an aspirational model but also, importantly, one which few students could identify with as it remains distant from their realities.

For me, the best way to adapt this was to maintain the concept of 'relaxing at home' but allow different narratives to appear alongside the Danish example. So, I chose voices from the **Global South**, non-English speaking countries and other diverse groups – older people, those from low-income families or other ethnicities.

The new images showed a wide selection of real homes from these different contexts, not stereotypical representations. In other words, a more modest home in Denmark alongside a modern, comfortable one found in a lower income country. Each text was of a similar length with a similar size image so that none was presented as a superior model. Finally, to make the whole lesson more authentic, I substituted the current text style (written in an objective journalistic tone) for real voices of different people talking about their homes (see **22**). I interviewed a number of friends or acquaintances for this.

This was a major adaptation and required some time and thought about how to make the lesson more inclusive. A lighter, and no less worthy approach, would be simply to maintain the text but allow the students to critique it in order to reveal its unspoken messages and then suggest alternatives themselves.

Example 2: 'Thanksgiving' (Lesson plan published online by Linguahouse.com)

My colleague Stephanie Hirschman was tasked with adapting an existing lesson plan about the American holiday Thanksgiving. The original text about the celebration focused, among other things, on the historical context. It referred to the 'local Native American people' who helped the Pilgrims when they arrived in 1620 by welcoming them and giving them food. This connection and the subsequent relationship between the two peoples was celebrated with a festival which became today's Thanksgiving holiday. The article in the original lesson referred only to Native Americans and Indians (both problematic terms) and did not mention a specific nation. It did not problematize Thanksgiving in any way and made no reference to any subsequent negative events. The website received a number of comments requesting an updated revision which included the Native American perspective.

Stephanie recognized that the text was written from the perspective of the Pilgrims and the benefit they received from the Native Americans without telling the story from the latter's point of view at all. In her adapted version, she referred to the Wampanoag nation by name and removed the term Indian, which some people have considered offensive. Then, in the final paragraph, she signposted the alternative point of view that **Indigenous** people have of this holiday:

'… the holiday is not without controversy and recent years have seen people consider how Native Americans view the holiday, as well as the impact on the environment of modern Thanksgiving celebrations.'

This provided a link to a new jigsaw reading activity which she added to the material. One text focused on climate change and the environmental impact of Thanksgiving, the other made explicit reference to the genocidal impact of European settlement of North America. She also included some disruptive questions for discussion of these texts. Here is part of the second additional text which focused on the festival's controversial identity:

'Even before 1620, Europeans had introduced diseases into North America which killed huge numbers of Native Americans, including many Wampanoag. Despite their alliance with the Pilgrims, over time the Wampanoag died in further epidemics, were sold into slavery and lost their lands. Again and again, Europeans made treaties with native people and then broke them, and this pattern was repeated all over the North American continent. It is hardly surprising that native peoples feel that Thanksgiving is a celebration of genocide. Native Americans from all over the country want the truth to be told about their history in general and about Thanksgiving in particular.'

By tweaking the original text and adding this new focus, Stephanie was able to add a different perspective without it dominating the main thrust of her material. This worked well because Thanksgiving had to be established as a topic in its own right before the inclusive reading could be introduced. The students have to learn the traditional story in order to then 'unlearn it'. She was pleased with the adaptation even though the prescribed length of the text couldn't accommodate inclusion of the voice of a member of the Native American community giving their opinion directly about the festival. The adaptation is also an excellent example of the publishers Linguahouse.com responding positively to user requests for a more inclusive reading.

Note: Though 'Native American' is used above in the adapted version, the term preferred by the Wampanoag themselves is 'Native People'.

https://www.linguahouse.com/esl-lesson-plans/general-english/thanksgiving

Bearing in mind the previous ideas, how can you guarantee that the materials you produce are accurate, authentic, representative and have genuine value?

Here are six key principles:

1   Tie materials to inclusive representation. This means that all identities, narratives and realities should be represented equitably and authentically and not be challenged. To do this, keep questions on **marginalized** identities factual to the content and avoid questions that ask learners to make value judgements. This can open the door to discriminatory remarks (see **15**) and is a way of reinforcing the dominant culture's voice. Also, be wary of asking questions which focus on differences between students and certain groups, as these can make assumptions about the learners' identities.

2   Consider the approach you take to represent these identities, narratives and realities. Seburn (2021, p. 60) suggests two key ways to achieve this representation: **usualization** and **disruption.** He defines *usualization* as representation 'without highlighting the specialness (or 'strangeness') of individuals from marginalized groups and to spread their narratives alongside all others with regular frequency.'

The advantage of usualization is students don't see the group as belonging to a special category, but something usual, even matter-of-fact. For example, consider a text in which five different people give their opinions about how they get around their city. One of the five happens to be in a wheelchair. Here, the wheelchair user is included, they are clearly visible to students, but no big deal is made about their identity (see **23** for extended examples).

Disruption, in some ways, takes an opposite approach. It includes identifying a marginalized group by focusing explicitly on an unfair social **norm** related to them (e.g. the fact that women do not hold top positions in most companies and are often paid less for doing the same job). The students critique this in class, are exposed to examples from those affected and then importantly, suggest steps to take action against this situation (e.g. challenge the pay structures in certain companies that allow this situation to perpetuate itself).

These different approaches have a great effect on how the materials are used in class. With the disruption approach, the teacher has to be prepared to make the unfair social norm or marginalized group a central focus of the lesson. However, if they feel that the environment in class is not conducive to discussing this topic at length, then it may be best avoided and a usualization approach adopted instead.

3   Consult authentic, real-life sources and make these the focus. In order to do this, you may need to do some research (see **23** for ideas on sourcing). For example, if you are focusing on a current humanitarian crisis, then going to a source such as Médecins Sans Frontières would be a good first step. Even so, it is always a good idea to consult multiple sources to get content double-checked. The other concern is the perspectives and voices represented in the sources. Rather than providing students with a text *about* a particular community written from an outsider's perspective, find one from an insider's viewpoint (see **20**). Sadly, most published materials still feature the outsider perspective, with the danger that this group is represented unfairly, inaccurately or inauthentically. It is always preferable to ground the material in the lived experience of somebody who belongs to this group or community. The phrase 'don't speak about us without us' is a good way to sum up this idea.

4   When giving the opinions of a group member, make sure these individuals are not seen as spokespeople for the group. This avoids the group being viewed in a stereotypical or one-dimensional way. As Seburn says, 'Individualism rather than generalization creates a more inclusive approach because we are, in fact, all different, and no one person can be the representative of an entire group' (ibid, p. 15).

Now, with regard to *use* in class …

5   Don't impose your own values or opinions in the materials. Likewise, do not ask leading questions which guide students to think in a particular way or assume that they will be surprised by something. The important thing is that you expose your students to a group which is often excluded or misrepresented in materials.

Once this is done, it is best for the students to come to their own conclusions about it. However, if these conclusions are not inclusive, then you should attempt to challenge them (see **15**).

6   Don't allow particular representations to make somebody reveal more about themselves than they wish. For example, if you have a wheelchair user in class who has read the text mentioned in point 2, you should avoid putting the spotlight on them unless, of course, they feel comfortable giving their opinion on this topic.

A case study

In an article from IATEFL Voices, Tania Pattison writes about producing materials about **Indigenous** children in Canada. The topic was on the curriculum, but she soon realized that it was one she didn't feel equipped to deal with (in particular with regard to The Truth and Reconciliation Commission which investigated the treatment of Indigenous children who were removed from their homes and placed in residential schools in the name of assimilation from 1876 to 1997 by the Canadian authorities).

Pattison (2021, p. 9) says: 'How could I work with this subject matter and produce material that was a) accurate b) sensitive and c) still pedagogically effective? I'm not indigenous. I'm not even Canadian. Could I write materials about this subject? Did I have any right to do so?'

In the end, she decided to go ahead but focus her materials on direct accounts given to the Commission when the children concerned were adults (see point 3 above). The article also gives useful advice on working with material of a similarly sensitive or traumatic nature. She suggests building in opportunities for individual reflection, allowing students flexibility in how to access the material and not sugar-coating it. Pattison says you have to consider your lived experience and **positionality** with regard to the content, and consider any preconceptions or **biases** you may have about it (see **5**, **11**). Fundamentally, and quite apart from the pedagogical and linguistic reasons for text choice, you have to ask yourself *why* you are using that material as this will inform how you approach it in class.

Pattison, T. (2021) Writing effective EAP Materials about traumatic subjects, *Voices*, Issue 283, Nov/Dec 2021, pp. 9–11.

Seburn, T. (2021) *How to Write Inclusive Materials*. ELT Teacher 2 Writer.

Stereotyping and othering in materials

We have seen that when looked at with a critical eye, apparently inclusive materials can be found to include stereotypical representations and/or 'other' identities and communities. Let's now look at these in more detail, identifying common stereotypes and what can be done to rectify them.

One way to understand the power of stereotyping is to do a simple speaking activity with your students:

Below are five behavioural traits, customs and characteristics. Would you say they are 1, individual (they apply to individual people), 2, cultural (they apply to any kind of cultural group) or 3, universal (they apply to us all). If cultural, which cultures come to mind – a country or a part of one, or another kind of cultural group?

1 Liking spicy food
2 Respecting elderly people
3 Leaving the window open when you sleep
4 Crossing the road only when you see the 'green man'
5 Smiling for the camera

This a typical critical thinking activity and, as such, there are no correct answers. However, when the answer involves discussion about a particular cultural group, it may well reveal certain stereotypes. I have heard students say that 'liking spicy food' applies to Thais, 'smiling broadly for the camera' to Brazilians because they like showing off their white teeth, and 'crossing the road when you see the green man' to Germans because they are disciplined and may tell you off if you don't do this.

It may be the case that some of these arguments are based on real experiences that some students have had, but equally these choices could be based on stereotypical impressions that students have heard via word-of-mouth, the media or representations in popular culture.

Problems arise if these stereotypical ideas really are sweeping generalizations, reductionist or harm the culture concerned. This is what we refer to as taking an *essentialist* attitude, adopting the belief that each of these cultural groups has an 'essential' or 'unchangeable' nature which explains their identity. It is this kind of stereotype that we want to avoid in learning materials because it gives the impression that different cultures can be 'explained away' by such fixed traits or characteristics.

Tony Malone (2022) in *The Diversity and Inclusion Glossary* (pp. 197–198) includes this in his definition of *stereotype*: 'Members of minority groups can sometimes be seen as deviant or threatening and subsequently stereotyped with negative characteristics – laziness or criminality for example. Even 'benign' stereotyping – as in the notions that all Asians are ambitious or that Muslim girls are passive – can be misleading and are damaging.'

Saying that 'Thai people like spicy food' may sound quite benign, certainly not as harmful as saying that 'Spanish people like bullfighting,' but these stereotypes betray the same essentialist agenda.

Identifying stereotypes

In order to dispel stereotypes, it is important to be able to identify them. Sadly, many of us are aware of the racist stereotypes that have been historically levelled at **People of Colour**. Stereotypes such as 'Black people are more likely to be involved in criminal activities, are not economically self-sufficient' and so on are particularly harmful. Even stereotypes which project seemingly positive traits such as athleticism can be limiting because they ignore the diversity of other talents and interests within the Black community (see **29**).

Some stereotypes can, however, be far harder to detect. Even decorative images can betray them. Recently, I saw a high-impact image used as the warmer page of a coursebook unit on Health Sciences. It showed two young Chinese women, one wearing a face mask and the other covering her mouth with her hand and looking scared. The warmer questions focused on different global health risks. These images thus reflected the stereotype that Chinese people are more concerned with health than others and take precautions. This may not seem a harmful stereotype, but it contributes to *othering*, treating a particular group of people as fundamentally different and alien to one's own group. This creates an 'us' v 'them' mindset.

Here is a short list of some common stereotypes (sadly there are many others) that our materials need to challenge. It is unlikely that materials these days will represent these stereotypes explicitly, but they still may appear implicitly or members of these communities may simply be erased altogether. The stereotypes are extremely harmful in their own right but more importantly, it is the effect these stereotypes have on our attitudes and actions that needs to be countered.

Women: they are solely responsible for domestic tasks and caregiving, are emotional or irrational, preoccupied with their physical appearance, financially dependent on men and unable to lead. These stereotypes can reinforce gender disparities and undermine women's credibility.

People with disabilities: they are helpless and dependent on others, need our pity rather than a recognition of their strengths and capabilities. These misconceptions and over generalizations lead many people to develop patronizing attitudes which can limit disabled people's opportunities. They are also often regarded as 'inspirational heroes' for simply living their lives or framed as exceptional such as when Paralympians are included. Although these are positive representations, these special cases do not represent a reality which most disabled people can relate to.

LGBTQIA+ community: stereotypes based on sexual orientation include that gay men are effeminate or that lesbians adhere to certain masculine traits. **Transgender** people may face stereotypes that question the validity of their identity, ignoring the existence of **non-binary** individuals. In popular culture, some LGBTQIA+ individuals face tragic endings because of the assumption that they cannot lead happy lives.

Case study: Helen Keller

Lottie Galpin told me about some stereotypical and ultimately harmful representations she had noted of famous disabled people. One example focused on texts or representations of Helen Keller, a writer, activist and educator who was deafblind. Representations of Keller often focus on her impairment and how she overcomes it in order to communicate. Ostensibly, these representations could seem positive in that they show a disabled person overcoming their impairment. But this is a simplistic reading.

Some representations show Keller as succeeding because of outside help, others show Keller as being responsible for her own success. However, both focus only on her impairment and success story, as if there was nothing else to her identity. This framing is problematic for various reasons. Firstly, by focusing on her impairment, Keller is set in the position of 'other', as outside the supposed non-disabled **norm**. Secondly, the representation of disabled people as overcoming adversity is obviously limiting and a stereotype. It is also an example of 'identity flattening', which is the reducing of a multifaceted identity to a one dimensional and less complex one. In the representations, there is little mention of her rich professional and private life.

Galpin pointed out that such texts would have worked much better if they had presented Keller as a nuanced and complex person and included other aspects of Keller's identity and lifestyle rather than reducing to just focusing on her disability (see **14**).

Malone, T. (2022) *The Diversity and Inclusion Glossary*. Pied Wagtail Publishing.

> Starting with some general advice, we then identify
> specific sources which you can turn to for inspiration.
> We finish with a positive example from one of the
> recommended sources.

If you need to source materials on topics outside your lived experience
or are writing about people whose identities are different from your
own, it is a good idea to research carefully before you start. By all
means seek out current news stories, but be sure that that they include
authentic voices and are not written from an outsider's perspective.
First-hand accounts can be also be sourced by accessing social media,
YouTube videos, charity websites and the following other sources.
However, another more direct approach is simply to ask people from
within the community via a general call for help on social media. In this
case, it is important not to rely on just one view: the more contacts you
can make, the more perspectives you will gather and the more balanced
your materials will be as a result (see Seburn, 2021).

Projects/Podcasts

The Hands-Up Project: This outstanding initiative involves remote
volunteers around the world and Palestine-based volunteers
running online, storytelling sessions for young learners (https://
www.handsupproject.org/). The project, 'affords opportunities for
children in difficult circumstances, such as Palestine, to use English
to communicate with one another across borders in a spirit of peace,
dignity, tolerance, freedom, equality and solidarity' (UNICEF, 1989).
The Project also runs free teacher development and storytelling
courses for Palestinian teachers. From the materials perspective, the
Project's website includes many children's stories which offer personal,
first-hand experiences of life in Gaza, **refugee** camps in Jordan and
elsewhere.

The ESOL Podcast: represents a space for ESOL students' voices to be heard (https://esolpodcast.co.uk). UK migrants share stories, talk about their everyday lives, impressions of the UK, tips for learning English, as well as engage in more profound discussions on topics such as the importance of community and belonging. The site features downloadable material that can be used with any of the available podcasts.

Story Corps: represents the largest single collection of human voices ever gathered (https://storycorps.org). Its thousands of stories – which can be heard in the form of podcasts or read via transcripts – are divided into collections such as 'American Pathways' and 'Parenthood Stories', and represent the diverse cultures of current American society through lived experiences. The stories told by people from different backgrounds and first languages offer interesting perspectives and viewpoints for the language classroom.

Videos

Stories that Move: a website that features video clips of **minority** teenagers from different parts of the world (https://www.storiesthatmove.org/en/). These videos, in interview format, are divided into five categories or learning paths: Seeing and Being (on identities), Facing Discrimination, Life Stories, Mastering the Media and Taking Action. The site includes an online toolbox – useful teacher resource materials including worksheets and educator guides. The videos are available in a number of languages including English, subtitles are also available in nine languages and therefore could easily be used in multiple language learning contexts (see **10**). The interviews also feature identities which are not always featured in inclusive materials – e.g. **Roma,** Jewish and Chinese.

DLA Vlogger Academy: a bank of over 60 graded videos made by real life vloggers from around the world. There is a strong emphasis on diverse voices and those often excluded from mainstream publishing (see below for focus on Wenzile). They can be viewed on Vimeo (https://vimeo.com/showcase/r2r-vlogs).

Texts/Print material

Raise Up for ELT: a multi-level coursebook series each containing eight lessons on a variety of subjects (https://raiseupforelt.com/resources/). The methodology and design reflect that normally found in international mainstream coursebooks, but the content is notably more inclusive. It thus provides teachers with practical, ready to use lessons that are genuinely diverse.

Existence: Eight LGBTQIA+ inclusive ELT resources (Fullagar, 2024): comprehensive and varied examples of LGBTQIA+ materials. Creative, critical and highly practical, these resources can be easily used in classrooms where a **safe space** has been created to discuss such identities.

Images

Here is a selection of online image banks which offer authentic alternatives to the archives most often used in published ELT materials. The five below feature images of many communities which are excluded and misrepresented in the mainstream: women, older people, **People of Colour** and people with disabilities among others. It is important to read the terms of use information carefully in all cases.

https://www.disabilityimages.com/
https://ageing-better.org.uk/news/age-positive-image-library-launched
https://jopwell.pixieset.com/thejopwellcollection/
https://www.wocintechchat.com/blog/wocintechphotos
https://www.pocstock.com//

Example of positive representation

Vlog: Wenzile: How Clothes Make Me Feel

This vlog features Wenzile Thwala a Black, **transgender** woman from Johannesburg and is titled 'How Clothes Make Me Feel' (accessible https://bcove.video/4g11VOV). In the three-minute vlog, Wenzile describes the importance of her clothes to her trans identity. She explains their role in expressing her individuality, of making her who she is and how she feels. Clothes provide her with a sense of belonging, reflect her moods and the different roles she adopts in life.

The strength of the material is that Wenzile comes across at all times as a relatable role model, she is simply 'one of us'. After all, you don't have to be Black or trans to relate to the topic of clothes and what they say about you. Her video is fundamentally about an exploration of her identity and sense of self. As such, she becomes somebody any viewer could, in theory, relate to or empathize with. Importantly, Wenzile's vlog appears alongside multiple other voices in DLA Vlogger's Academy and I think it would be ideally shown alongside another of these videos so that the class does not become just a lesson about trans identities.

The methodology adopted in this example follows a **usualization** approach to inclusive content (see **21**). The 'specialness' of the narrative is not referred to explicitly. We know and can see for ourselves that Wenzile is a transgender woman from Johannesburg but her status is not the be-all and end-all. Her words are presented alongside others in the Academy and there is no attempt to present this material as 'difficult' or 'different' to any of the other voices or videos in which these narratives are contextualized.

However, it is equally important that if students wish to investigate the topic of transgender identity in more depth and discuss it explicitly then they should be allowed to do so. The extent to which this happens, of course, will depend on the context in which the material is used, the profile of the learners and their relationship with each other and their teacher.

Regarding inclusive representation, I believe that all of the above resources include materials which fulfill Seburn's (2021) criteria (see **21**):

1   Members of minority groups are represented with regularity alongside other narratives.
2   Authentic voices should be consulted and inform narrative creation.
3   Members of minority groups are represented as individuals, not as a collective whole.

Fullagar, P. J. (2024) *Existence: Eight LGBTQIA+ inclusive ELT resources.* Peter J. Fullagar.

Seburn, T. (2021) *How to Write Inclusive Materials.* ELT Teacher 2 Writer.

UNICEF (1989) *Convention on the Rights of the Child.* https://www.unicef.org/child-rights-convention/convention-text

E: Assessment

Clearly, assessment is only valid if it is fair and inclusive. A candidate's results should never be influenced by their identity or circumstances. This section looks at these ethical issues as well as practical preparations and adjustments that can be made to make the assessment process as equitable as possible.

Thanks to Pablo Toledo for his advice on this section.

The Universal Design for Learning (CAST, 2024) is based around providing multiple means of representation, engagement and action and expression (see 7). These principles are a good starting point for establishing inclusive test design, conditions and procedures.

In the case of *representation*, consider the way test items are presented. Do any create barriers for students? For example, some **neurodiverse** students may not respond well to long multiple-choice questions with no visuals. In the case of *action and expression*, consider ways in which students will respond and demonstrate their knowledge in a test. Do they need to organize information mentally, or can something be provided to help them, such as a digital aid? Finally, in the case of *engagement*, consider the problem of multi-tasking and don't set tasks which require students to listen and read or write at the same time whilst doing a test.

Practical guidelines

The UDL (CAST, 2015) have also specified practical tips and guidelines regarding test design and test conditions. Here is a summary of these:

Test design

Simple, clear and intuitive instructions and procedures

Assessment instructions (both spoken and written) and rubrics should be easy to understand, regardless of a student's experience, knowledge, language skills, or concentration level. Directions and questions need to be in simple and concise language tied to the test's learning goal. In this way, test takers can respond as the test developers intended. If using technical terms or acronyms, use glossaries to guarantee understanding.

Maximum readability, comprehensibility and legibility

These guidelines, aimed mainly at neurodiverse students, of course, would apply when creating any language materials but are doubly important in an assessment as the stakes are raised substantially. Adopting this advice has the additional advantage that the tests are easier on the eye for all students.

Readable fonts

- Use sans serif fonts, such as Arial or Calibri (rather than, for example, Times New Roman).
- Ideally, font size should be 12–14 point. For headings, use a font size that is 20 percent larger.
- Avoid underlining and italic; it can make the text run together.
- Use bold for emphasis.
- Avoid using uppercase letters for continuous text.
- Add extra space around headings and between paragraphs.

Colour

- Use single colour backgrounds. Off-white or cream is a good choice as plain white can appear too bright.
- Avoid background patterns or pictures and distracting surrounds.
- Avoid green and red/pink, as these colours are difficult for those with dyslexia and/or colour vision deficiencies.

Layout

- Align text to the left and without justification. This makes it easier to find the start and finish of each line.
- Make sure there is even spacing between words.
- Use additional white space around text and regular section headings for reading ease.

Style

- Avoid long dense paragraphs.
- Consider using bullet points and numbering rather than continuous text.
- Use images to support text.
- Flow charts are good for explaining procedures.

- Pictograms or graphs can help to locate and support information in the text. These should be of an appropriate size with any labels or captions clearly visible. However, avoid purely decorative images which draw attention away from the test content itself.

Format

In general, consider providing different formats for displaying information. Tables, charts, infographics rather than plain text may be more accessible. Think too about embedding extras in digital assessments such as text-to-speech capability, key word definitions, hints or coaching tips, etc. so students feel supported (see **14**).

Precisely defined constructs

Well-designed assessments must measure what they are intended to measure and offer the greatest opportunity for success within those constructs. Universally-designed assessments should remove as many cognitive, sensory, emotional and physical barriers as possible. However, by their very nature, many will include features that are not directly related to the construct and often require additional skills and processing. These are considered to be 'construct irrelevant' elements. For example, a test which used unfamiliar vocabulary, cultural references or idiomatic expressions unrelated to the construct would be considered construct irrelevant. It may not be possible to eradicate all of these elements but, as a general rule, look for and remove any barriers that do not coincide with the learning goals you want to measure.

Accessible, non-biased items

Procedures need to be put in place to analyse assessment content for **bias**, stereotyping and **tokenism.** A lack of sensitivity towards any group should be identified and corrected as it would be with any language teaching materials (see **22**).

Test conditions: Open to adjustments or access arrangements

There are many possible adjustments or access arrangements that can be made to a test to make it inclusive:

- extra time (25 percent is often stipulated) for previewing questions and items
- supervised rest breaks

- a separate room either in a small group or alone (particularly useful for students with **autism**)
- change of seating arrangement
- use of a reader or a scribe
- use of a prompter to keep students focused
- use of a computer or digital device instead of pen and paper
- use of digital tools (screen reader/voice recognition software, etc.)
- use of exam papers in different formats (e.g. digital).

Within a formative assessment framework, it is a good idea to provide flexible options so that students can choose the questions they feel they can answer to the best of their ability (see **8**). If the answer demands a more creative response, students could produce a video or an audio or use speech-to-text software (see **12**) rather than write text themselves.

If you vary these possible assessment formats over a period of time, students are likely to be more motivated and engaged as a result. Be open, in particular, to the students' own suggestions about how they can best tackle a test. For example, if they have the flexibility to provide shorter responses or choose task types such as matching or underlining tasks rather than gap-fills, then all the better.

Many assessment programmes now use these elements to an extent and students with disabilities are frequently consulted to help with design. Indeed, if a student shows a preference for any other of the above adjustments and/or suggests others, then do follow their advice where possible.

Exam boards publish their approaches and accommodations, for example:
- Cambridge Assessment provide ample guidance notes on special requirements for official exams: https://www.cambridgeenglish.org/help/special-requirements/
- Cambridge International Exams offer past papers in suitable formats for neurodiverse and visually impaired students: https://www.cambridgeinternational.org/exam-administration/cambridge-exams-officers-guide/phase-1-preparation/access-arrangements/.

They are also starting to incorporate choice in general exam design. One example is the Cambridge IGCSE Science qualification. Here, candidates can either carry out a practical test or take an alternative paper if they are unable to do experiments in a laboratory.

- See also a Cambridge online article on advantages of digital exams: https://www.cambridge.org/elt/blog/2024/03/07/advantages-of-digital-exams-for-accessibility-and-inclusivity/.

If a student is due to take an official exam, make sure to check out well in advance the access arrangements available. For example, Cambridge allows students to request extra time for their exams beforehand. Such requests should be made six weeks before the test in the case of IELTS (https://ielts.org/take-a-test/booking-your-test/access-arrangements).

Case study: Cambridge English Qualifications Digital platform

Let's now take a look at the accessibility features of the Cambridge English Qualifications Digital platform as an example:

On the platform, candidates have control over the text size themselves. They can easily change between regular, large and extra-large text size, without the need for extra equipment. Likewise, learners with visual stress, dyslexia, moderately low vision or impaired contrast perception can benefit from enhancing the text control. The default is black text on a white background but candidates can choose to change this either to white text on a black background or yellow text on a black background. Volume control can also be adjusted easily, as each candidate has their own set of headphones. All candidates also have the advantage of typing their answers rather than writing them by hand, allowing them to edit their work more easily. Finally, with regard to ease of navigation, candidates answer each question on screen where the question is asked, eliminating the need to transfer answers. In addition, the navigation bar at the bottom makes it easy to move around between questions if needed. For learners with fine motor or visual impairments, most of this navigation can be done with the keyboard rather than the mouse, for example, by using the tab key to move to the next field.

CAST (2024) *Universal Design for Learning Guidelines version 3.0.* Retrieved from https://udlguidelines.cast.org

CAST (2015) *Top 10 UDL Tips for Assessment.* https://slds.osu.edu/posts/documents/top-10-udl-tips.pdf

First, we will look at the preparations needed for students taking formal exams, then at the adjustments that may need to be made. Finally, we will discuss the benefits of formative in-class assessments for inclusive practice.

Assessment *of* learning: Preparations

Some points here have been adapted from: https://blog. cambridgeinternational.org/top-tips-for-supporting-students-with-send-before-and-during-exams/.

Before an external exam or formal assessment, **disabled** and **neurodiverse** students may experience problems with planning and organization including memorizing techniques and prioritizing information. Therefore, they may require additional support in these areas during their preparation. The tips below should, in any case, benefit all students.

Revision techniques

Help students organize their revision by creating relevant folders for their work as well as study schedules and time organizers. Make these as visually appealing as possible, using highlighters to make different sections stand out. In terms of the content to revise, break it down into chunks using mind-maps, sub-headings and bullet points.

Encourage students to write summaries or get those with literacy or attention difficulties to make oral versions or voice notes using their digital devices. If taking past papers, ask students to reflect on their experience by recording it in a journal. Any kind of journal or diary can help students think about the areas that they still need to work on or the steps required to achieve their learning goals.

Focus students' attention on different ways to retain information including looking at illustrations, images, photos of written information taken on a digital device as well as songs and memory aids. Encourage your students individually to think about how best they work, what makes them feel most comfortable and able to absorb information efficiently. This could include their ideal time of day for study, what environment they work best in, whether to study alone or with a friend or which strategies can best help them (see **24**).

Exam techniques

Highlight the importance of reading questions properly. Encourage students, especially those who may struggle with reading skills, to re-read questions a number of times before answering. Teach students to focus on the key words that clarify the meaning of a question and show them techniques in how to eliminate distractors in multiple choice questions. Be sure to go over the key verbs used in instructions such as *describe*, *compare*, *evaluate*, *discuss*, etc. to avoid confusion. Provide practice in proofreading by going through an example yourself so that students familiarize themselves with this important skill.

Students often find timing difficult and do not like the idea of leaving a question without finishing it and moving on to the next. Explain that it is normal to leave questions and return to them later, as we all sometimes need extra time to reflect on our answers.

Interestingly, the Covid pandemic (2020–2022) showed us how possible it was to break down some of these barriers by taking an anticipatory approach. For example, with regard to timing, students were given take-home exams on a lockdown browser which meant they could take the exam anytime over a 24-hour period. It would be a good option to revert to these kinds of digital adjustments where practically viable.

Mental health

Exam preparation is, of course, a stressful time for everybody. However, for students with disabilities it can just intensify difficulties that they may already have. Make sure that you let all students know that anxieties are normal and that you are available for any support they might need. If viable, giving prompts and encouragement during the assessment might alleviate some of that anxiety.

The typical exam room can be a particularly overwhelming place. Although it may smack of segregation, consider an alternative venue for some students if that is a practical option. In any case, invite students to visit the room beforehand and familiarize themselves with it. This will help them visualize how they may feel on the day of the exam and reflect on what they will need to do when there.

Assessment *for* learning: Peer and self-assessment

We have focused on ways to prepare for formal summative assessment as that is an everyday reality that many of us face. However, critics have accused such assessments of 'becoming pedagogical tools of **exclusion** ... privileging the value of certain knowledge systems, abilities, behaviors and skills over others ... focusing on what students can't do rather than ... thinking about what they bring to the assessment process' (Payne, 2023). This perspective that emphasizes students' deficits rather than acknowledging their assets is known as *the deficit discourse* and is prevalent in the design of summative exams.

Formative assessment or assessment for learning, on the other hand, is centred on growth and development within the classroom, and thus can more easily involve learners in the process. This adds coherence and consistency to assessment procedure, as decisions can be made mutually. Students will clearly feel more included if the goals, learning processes and evaluation criteria are 'harmonized' in this way.

One way to embrace this greater inclusion is to offer greater opportunities for self- and peer-assessment. Both are inclusive because they provide students with agency, encouraging them to evaluate progress on their own terms and feedback on assessment content and policy. This is important because evaluation criteria are often established externally, particularly in high stakes summative assessment, in which a one size fits all approach is followed (see **26**).

Benefits of in-class testing

In the long term, the solution to inclusive assessment may lie in simply reducing the amount of formal testing offered, as it is far easier to include adjustments in classroom-based tests. Rather than have students present live PowerPoints in front of the class, students could be given a number of options, e.g. choosing to do the test one-to-one, with their group or with only the teacher present, in a different room, recording it beforehand or even reducing the time of the presentation (see **24**).

In any case, if your institution intends to retain some formal assessment, there are a number of things to consider when practising in class. Firstly, it is important to ensure that the format and content of questions and task types seen in class are similar to those found in formal exams, so there are no surprises on 'the big day'. This reduces anxiety and fear of the unexpected and helps students become assessment literate, demystifying the high-stakes exam to an extent.

This practice is also best done in class where the students can develop the skills needed for summative assessment and discuss strategies with their colleagues and yourself. This should allow for more risk-taking, as students will be able to build confidence together (see **24**).

The other advantage of including these kinds of assessment type tasks in class is that you are able to give students immediate feedback (again important for neurodiverse students and/or those who may have low self-esteem). Such feedback should emphasize what the student can do in the moment rather than what they are not yet able to do, focusing particularly on the use of newly acquired language. If possible, try to avoid providing a grade as shifting students' attention away from marking reduces competition. The Center for Assessment have produced an interesting evaluative framework for creating accessible and inclusive formative assessments: https://www.nciea.org/blog/a-culturally-responsive-classroom-assessment-framework/

Payne, S. (2023) Ask the Experts: Becoming an assessment JEDI (Cambridge Assessment Network webinar) https://learning.canetwork.org.uk/mod/book/view.php?id=4385&chapterid=5093 (script and video accessed 29.12.24)

26 Fair and ethical assessment

> Discussions of fairness and inclusion are now central to current debates on assessment. The responsibilities of testers and the rights of test takers are the main concerns here.

The idea that language testing should be understood within a broader societal context has come to the fore partly because of the status and role of large-scale summative assessments which dominate language education policy. Seen through a social justice lens (see **6**), this form of assessment can be seen both as systemically unfair and a means to reinforce dominant cultures. In some cases, these tests are imposed by governments or other powerful organizations and test takers have been given little choice but to comply with the testing demands.

For example, for **immigrants** who move to countries where English is the dominant language and medium of instruction, passing citizenship tests may include academic content which represents a major challenge as the test takers are still in the process of acquiring the new language. In most countries where English is not the dominant language, passing a high-stakes English test is also compulsory to graduate from high school and enter higher education.

Academics, such as Elana Shohamy (2022, p. 1,448) in her work on Critical Language Testing (CLT), have emphasized the misuse of such forms of assessment and the potential harm and **exclusion** they can cause, 'The issues [are] not whether language tests are good or bad from a perspective of accuracy … but rather about giving attention to the impact of tests on people and the need to monitor their uses.' Seen from this perspective, the goal of testing should be to ensure their ethicality and fairness.

Ethical issues in testing thus encompass two major dimensions: 1) the quality of test items designed by language testers and 2) the factors influencing the use and outcomes of the tests. Regarding terminology, McNamara and Ryan (2011, p. 161) have differentiated between the fairness which they understand to be related to a test's technical qualities and justice which 'encompasses the values implicit in test constructs, and the social uses to which language tests may be put'.

Codes of practice and ethics

To this end, language test developers and associations of language testers have introduced and frequently updated codes of practice and ethics which define the responsibilities and obligations of language testers and test takers. For example, the ILTA's (International Language Testing Association) Guidelines of Practice (updated in 2020) is divided into three parts. Part 1 covers basic considerations for good testing practice in all test/assessment situations. Part 2 covers the rights and responsibilities of test takers and Part 3 outlines specific considerations for classroom-based language assessment.

Apart from establishing guidelines for guaranteeing a test's validity and reliability, there are a number of important points made here with regard to inclusive practice: for example, the guidelines referring to the use of test results for decision making. Teachers should be prepared to explain and provide evidence of the fairness and accuracy of this decision-making process.

ILTA's Code of Ethics (updated 2018, p. 2) has an even more inclusive focus and is based around nine key principles. For example, it stipulates that, 'Language testers shall not discriminate against nor exploit their test takers on grounds of age, **gender,** race, **ethnicity,** sexual orientation, language background, creed, political affiliations or religion, nor knowingly impose their own values (for example social, spiritual, political and ideological), to the extent that they are aware of them.'

The ETS guidelines for Fair Tests and Communications (2022) are also of great practical use for inclusive practice. Here there is a major emphasis on the interpretation and use of test results and the expected profile of the test takers. The guidelines also establish the need for the pool of test writers and reviewers to be as diverse as possible.

The guidelines (p. 12), which establish a close link between fairness and validity, define fairness 'as the extent to which inferences and actions based on test scores are valid for a diverse population of test takers.'

The ETS' five general principles for establishing fairness are:

1 Measure the important aspects of the intended construct.
2 Provide scores that are valid for different groups in the intended population of test takers.
3 Treat all test takers respectfully and impartially.
4 Avoid barriers to the success of test takers, including those with disabilities and English-language learners.
5 Avoid content that raises strong negative feelings in test takers or others who are concerned about test materials (see **13**).

The final principle also includes many of the points we saw in materials (see **D**), focusing on the importance of inclusive language, the representation of diversity and the avoidance of stereotyping.

Multilingualism

One area of interest in Critical Language Testing has been the use of multilingual tests. Considering that translanguaging is now having an impact on ELT methodology and classroom management (see **10**), it follows that it should also have an impact on assessment design. For example, in some American states such as California, bilingual Spanish/English speakers are often wrongly labelled (see **3**) English Language Learner (ELL) or Long-Term English Learners (LTEL) because they score below average grades in official English standards-based achievement tests. As the tests are designed for monolingual speakers, some bilinguals may lack the literacy skills in English to pass and hence become stigmatized still further. If test contents were rethought to include the whole language repertoire of its test takers, these students would clearly benefit. Indeed, the presence of Spanish in such an exam would be symbolic because it would shift the focus from it being seen as a barrier to learning English.

In a similar vein, Shohamy (2001) has commented on research where two versions of a test – one bilingual and one monolingual – were used with 11th grade students of Russian origin in Israel. The results showed a clear advantage for the students who completed the bilingual (Hebrew-Russian) version compared to those immigrants who took the monolingual Hebrew-only version.

Final thoughts

Scott et al. (2014) conducted research related to fairness and equity in student assessment in Alberta, Canada. Although rather narrow and specific in scale and range, the key principles that emerged from the study are worth mentioning as a way to sum up this topic. These principles are that:

1 Educators must strive to understand and address the personal impact of assessment practices on individual students and their families.
2 Assessment must be differentiated to accommodate the ability, social, cultural and linguistic background of every student.
3 All members of school communities must challenge the complacency associated with accepting indefensible and illogical assessment practices.
4 The frequency, intensity and intrusiveness of assessments must not be overwhelming for students and their families.
5 Assessment must not be confused as a mechanism to counter inappropriate student behaviour or reward desired behaviour.

What underpins this research is the need to keep the student at the centre of the assessment process as well as to reinforce the core value of respect for the dignity and well-being of all those being assessed.

ETS (2022) *ETS Guidelines for Developing Fair Tests and Communications.* https://www. ets.org/pdfs/about/fair-tests-and-communications.pdf

ILTA Code of Ethics (2018) accessible https://www.iltaonline.com/page/CodeofEthics

ILTA Guidelines of Practice (2020) accessible https://www.iltaonline.com/page/ ILTAGuidelinesforPractice

McNamara, T. and Ryan, K. (2011) Fairness Versus Justice in Language Testing: The Place of English Literacy in the Australian Citizenship Test. *Language Assessment Quarterly* Volume 8, Issue 2

Scott, S., Webber, C. F., Lupart, J. L., Aitken, N. and Scott, D. E. (2014) Fair and equitable assessment practices for all students. *Assessment in Education: Principles, Policy & Practice*, 21(1), 52–70. https://doi.org/10.1080/0969594X.2013.776943

Shohamy, E. (2001) *The Power of Tests: A critical perspective on the uses of language tests.* London: Pearson.

Shohamy, E. (2022) Critical Language Testing, Multilingualism and Social Justice. *TESOL Quarterly*, Dec 2022. Open Access, https://onlinelibrary.wiley.com/doi/full/10.1002/ tesq.3185

F: Working together

Inclusive practice cannot work on a large scale if all stakeholders are not convinced of its benefits. This section looks at how involving colleagues, parents/ guardians, leaders and the extended community can help a teaching institution develop to become an inclusive space.

Giving and getting support from colleagues

Schools do not become equitable institutions by default nor are inclusive practices learned without determination and hard work. They can only become so through combined effort and the support of colleagues.

Within your institution there may well be teachers who do little or nothing to promote inclusive education policies. There may be others who say that they care and empathize but are reluctant to change their way of doing things. For meaningful change to take place, the institution as a whole has to question common practice based on dominant culture **norms** (see **6**). As Aow, Hollins and Whitehead (2023, p. 177) say: 'Understanding the key issues and gathering data to not only identify the problems that exist but also inspire and initiate meaningful change is essential.' By 'data', the authors here mean 'voices, stories, observations and experiences' which they suggest should be used alongside quantifiable data from surveys and so on.

As inclusion as a topic is not always covered in teacher training programmes, it is therefore a good idea to organize presentations or meetings with colleagues when possible. If your institution has established a whole school approach to inclusive practice, then these meetings could be the time to discuss its practical application and check that its principles are being adopted consistently. Here are some ideas for the content or direction of these meetings.

Using training sessions to grasp concepts

For teachers who are less experienced in inclusive practice, it may be necessary to provide extra support by way of training sessions. For example, to check teachers' prior knowledge, it could be useful to ask a series of questions about recognizing difference, **disability** or disadvantage. Alternatively, ask teachers to work with different frameworks so that they can more fully understand the challenges that certain students may face.

One useful training idea is to classify students' differences into categories and then ask teachers to think of particular challenges and decide which category they may belong to. While doing the task, emphasize that students can belong to multiple groups. It is also important to point out that any form of categorization is necessarily simplistic and potentially essentialist. However, presenting teachers with these categories of diversity (see **1**) from the School of Education at American University (2023) is as good a starting point as any: 1 Ability, 2 Age, 3 Gender, 4 Ethnic, 5 Religious, 6 Socio-economic, 7 Experiential, 8 Sexual Orientation, 9 Geographic.

It is important to expose teachers to this broad range of categories, as some are often ignored in EDI departments such as socio-economic, experiential or geographic diversity and their related challenges may not be immediately obvious. For example, challenges related to socio-economic diversity could include housing security/stability and precarious working conditions.

Sharing experiences/Case studies

More informal meetings (either virtual or face-to-face) would be ideal for sharing experiences and practical teaching techniques. For example, you could discuss common classroom management techniques, different interaction patterns (group work, pair work, etc.) and the advantages of each for **neurodiverse** students or those with physical disability. The strategies adopted will, of course, depend on your learner profiles. For instance, for teen classes, you might need to discuss different approaches to maintaining discipline or controlling bullying and so on. Teachers could also meet informally to share experiences about dealing with certain students in the form of case studies. These could either be descriptions of individual learners (possibly invented) or **critical incidents** in class that teachers could respond to (e.g. *This is what happened in my class. What would you have done in this case?*). Both are useful points of departure for awareness raising.

Discussing use of language

There are many issues surrounding the appropriate language to use in different situations. For example, amongst teachers it may be useful to refer to students as having **ADHD** but with parents and even the students themselves it would almost certainly be better to paraphrase the label and say something like, 'X or Y seems to get easily distracted'. Likewise, the language used to address students directly could be discussed, for example, the avoidance of expressions such as *you guys* or the recommended use of the *they* pronoun to refer to **non-binary** students (see **6**).

Action research projects

Continuous Professional Development (CPD) can also be achieved through action research projects which are often best undertaken by teachers in groups. Once an area of inclusive practice has been chosen (e.g. dealing with students who identify as non-binary) and different issues related to it have been discussed, certain strategies could be adopted.

Kemmis and McTaggart (adapted from Smith and Rebolledo, 2018) suggest this practical action research model: 1 develop a plan of critically informed action to improve what is already happening; 2 act to implement the plan; 3 observe the effects of the action in context; 4 reflect and interpret on these effects as the basis for planning more actions through a succession of stages.

These strategies are then tried out actively in the classroom and their effectiveness discussed and any modifications made. The findings from these projects are then shared with and evaluated by other teachers and final decisions taken about which strategies or techniques should be adopted.

One important thing to consider when we report on research is the ethical issues involved and the need to respect the rights of those participating even if the research findings are kept within the institution. Remember not to post photos or videos of children for the public without full consent from parents or guardians or of adult students without their consent. Informed and written consent is a general ethical requirement in any research. If you quote students, make sure these are not identifiable by other participants. Also bear in mind any personal information that you have collected from participants and the institution and whether this is relevant to include or can be made anonymous. There is also the broader issue of data protection. You should find out the details of your institution's ethics policy if it has one.

Sharing stories

A good way to introduce inclusion to teachers who are new to the concept is via storytelling. In particular, sharing students' own stories can be particularly enlightening as stories introduce an important human touch, arousing empathy, affinity, cooperation and connections. An excellent resource in this respect is Stories that Move, an 'online toolbox' for teaching about diversity and discrimination, guided by young people's real stories and experiences (see **23**). Alongside the videos are materials and useful teacher guides which would help colleagues get to grips with difficult and possibly triggering situations and may even make them question their own relationship with the topics addressed, for example, discrimination against LGBTQIA+, Muslim and **Roma** community, **antisemitism** and **racism**. Of course, you can also encourage your colleagues to share their own stories or those of their own learners. Cultivating safe, interactive spaces to do so is fundamental.

Aow, A., Hollins, S. and Whitehead, S. (2023) *Becoming a Totally Inclusive School: A Guide for Teachers and School Leaders.* Routledge.

Kemmis, S. and McTaggart, R. (1988) *The Action Research Planner* (3rd Ed.). Geelong: Deakin University.

Smith, R. and Rebolledo, P. (2018) *A Handbook for Exploratory Action*, British Council. Accessible: pub_30510_BC Explore Actions Handbook ONLINE AW-2.pdf (25)

Stories that Move: Toolbox against discrimination https://www.storiesthatmove.org/en/

School of Education, American University *Diversity in the Classroom: Teaching, Types, and Examples* https://soeonline.american.edu/blog/diversity-in-the-classroom/ (accessed 29.12.24)

> An inclusive education system requires the help of the
> entire community. It should also embody the principles
> of dialogue, participation and openness, bringing all
> stakeholders together to resolve any emerging tensions.

An important consideration here is that any institution's official
statements must be backed up by the way the institution is run and
organized. As Aow, Hollins and Whitehead (2023, pp. 89–90) say,
'There is no use in saying that it is within a school's mission to
promote diversity and inclusion, when there is a lack of diversity on
executive boards and in leadership teams.' They go on to say that a
'culture of care asks us at all levels of the school to be self-reflective
and understand the motivations underpinning the work being done.' In
general, schools, staff and curriculum should not be a mirror reflecting
back the views of dominant cultures.

An institution should therefore understand that diversity within its
teaching staff is a clear way to enhance inclusive practice, as these
teachers can bolster inclusion by serving as empathic role models
to all students. For example, it is crucial for an institution to recruit
teachers fairly, basing their criteria for selection on proficiency
and experience and not whether the candidate is a native speaker.
Indeed, many employers currently exclude highly qualified non-
native candidates because they inaccurately equate high CEFR levels
(C1 or C2) with "near-native" or "native-level" proficiency. The use
of such labels and their implied equivalence is both confusing and
discriminatory (see 3).

Raising awareness

Each institution implements its policies in different ways. However,
most should at the very least include a code of conduct or overall
school plan. If this document does not include any mention of inclusive
practice, then it is a good idea to try and lobby for change. Sending

that feedback to the school management or board via official channels is probably the first step to implementing new procedures. However, organizing petitions and campaigns requires both a good deal of time and a level of commitment so it would be valuable if specific teachers were made responsible for this and, if possible, were remunerated for their efforts.

A further way to start raising awareness within your school is via grassroots actions or events. Suggested activities could be performances, informative talks, panel discussions or debates from members of the community who represent diverse voices. This is much easier to do in collaboration with other teachers (see 27) as this work is done on a voluntary basis and, if not, may put additional pressure on individual teachers. It is important, however, that these actions are not just one-off, standalone events, that they represent a real cross-section of the local community and that the focus of the talks is positive and not just one of pain and trauma.

If inclusive policies are not applied within your school, it may well be because the institution does not consider its educators qualified enough to introduce them. If that is the case, it would be a good idea to convince your institution's management team to invest in teaching training sessions on inclusive practice. It would be even better if a member or members of the teaching staff were given the responsibility of organizing these. Continuous Professional Development (CPD) of this kind is particularly important in the case of inclusive practice as how it is interpreted changes rapidly and input needs updating. Additionally, it would be a good idea for these sessions to focus not just on pedagogic concerns but on broader issues outside the classroom. For example, it may be important to broaden understanding of what constitutes a marginalized group or highlight that there may be resistance and indeed opposition to inclusive practice within the community itself.

You may be thinking that a lot of this awareness raising requires time and effort, but it is also possible to do a lot in this field with only a little if you have the will to bring about change. As Helen Clark (2020, p. 8) says in her introduction to UNESCO's Global Education Report – Inclusion in Education: All Means All: 'Many changes can be made for free, in gestures made by teachers, in the ethos school leaders create for their learning environments, in the way families make decisions when school choices are presented to them, and in what we, as a society, decide we want for our future.'

Interacting with parents/guardians

In the case of primary and secondary education, parents are well placed to know the needs of their children and young people and to assess the school's inclusive policies with respect to them. They can support teachers with valuable information about their family background and history which may help explain the child's behaviour in class, a practice which can also make parents feel listened to and respected. Their specific observations from home together with a teacher's experience in class will help address barriers that the student may face (see **2**). This can be particularly helpful in the case of **neurodiverse** students or those with disabilities.

Parents and guardians value this school-home communication highly and it is common practice for schools to organize events and face-to-face meetings with teachers. Indeed, this is necessary so access to information about the school's organization and requirements is made available and their children's achievements and challenges are made apparent. Parents and guardians can also help reinforce the school programme through activities at home. This communication also benefits the students as they can see that the institution is working to support their needs. Teachers should, however, be prepared for some disagreements from parents and guardians, and strategies for defusing conflict should be employed where necessary.

It is, of course, desirable for parents and guardians to play an active role in the school's inclusive practice. Their participation in school activities and decision-making bodies such as school committees or boards is an important first step. However, this can often be challenging, either because parents are marginalized themselves or because of factors related to time, distance and language among others. For example, 'a study showed that most immigrant parents in the province of Quebec, Canada, were not involved in school committees due to work or their perception that the school was unapproachable and remote from their lives' (UNESCO, 2020, p. 188).

A teacher's anecdote

The greater part of this book has been directed at you the teacher and what you can do to help make your school a more inclusive space. The focus has chiefly been on how to make your students feel included and safe in class. But what about us teachers and our need to have our identities validated within an institution? For that reason, I want to end with a positive anecdote from a fellow teacher about how their overall well-being and relationship with their school altered as the result of a major change of policy at a government level.

My first teaching post was in a UK inner-city school, overwhelmingly made up of white students and staff. I was the only Black (male) teacher, and as such I was treated as something of an anomaly and curiosity. Fortunately (or not), I also happened to be the PE teacher so my Black identity fitted the dominant stereotype of all Black people being good at sport – though this alone didn't spare me the racist comments and innuendos, from both colleagues and students. I managed to acquire some validation of my personal and professional self through the success of our sports teams – but there was no chance of me being considered for a more senior position and my working life was not that pleasant. I was seen as the Black PE teacher and that was it.

And then an amazing thing happened – the city education authorities (who to be fair were quite enlightened on racial matters) appointed a female Black headteacher. Overnight my status and relationship to the school changed. Not only were there now two Black teachers in the school; the school was led by a Black woman. No longer was I the outsider (well, not as much as I had been), and at least I could now see a career pathway open up for me. That was a big turning point in my sense of wellbeing at that school and actually in my career in education from then on (Aow, et al., 2023, pp. 105–106).

Aow, A., Hollins, S. and Whitehead, S. (2023) *Becoming a Totally Inclusive School: A Guide for Teachers and School Leaders*. Routledge.

UNESCO (2020) Global Education Monitoring Report: https://unesdoc.unesco.org/ark:/48223/pf0000373878

How does an institution *know* if it is making advances in becoming a more inclusive space? Here we look at how a school can best evaluate its development and action according to key criteria and initiatives.

One of the problems with making changes at this level is that the goals for becoming an inclusive institution may be merely aspirational in order to pay lip service to EDI directives. Another important issue is that an institution's responses should be *anticipatory* and not reactionary. Switching to an anticipatory approach is crucial to fostering a sense of belonging and inclusion for all. This means making EDI policies and practices explicit and proactive. This can be done, for instance, by establishing training programmes where teachers and other stakeholders can become aware of the barriers faced by students and attempt to break them down (see **2** and **28**).

A self-assessment framework

Aow, Hollins and Whitehead (2023) have developed a helpful self-assessment framework for schools which outlines six stages of development that an institution could potentially go through in its journey from the discriminatory stage (1) to the totally inclusive stage (6) and the possible initiatives to take at each step along the way. The framework's six stages are categorized by:

1   Descriptors which focus on behaviours and mindsets, systems or structures which are typically found at the school.
2   Practices from the local community which focus on the kinds of things that educators there may say and the policies and infrastructure which may be in place.

The authors stress that making connections between these descriptors and practices and each institution's particular context is critical to success.

There is not sufficient space here to go into detail about these six stages, but I have included some examples from the final **Stage 6: 'An equitable and just institution'**. It is useful to look at in detail as it shows what an inclusive school can resemble and how it can affect the wider community on so many levels.

Stage 6: 'An equitable and just institution'

1 Descriptors

Behaviours and mindsets
Student/Staff voices, including those in historically oppressed groups, are intentionally integrated into the decision-making process.

Systems/Structures

[The school] implements structures, policies and practices with inclusive decision-making and other forms of power sharing at all levels of school life.

2 Practices from the learning community

What educators may say
'Let's slow down and look at this from multiple angles before we proceed.'

Policies and infrastructure

Teaching teams are varied, and contributions to curriculum design include diverse perspectives. Educators are aware of representation issues and engage in ways to expand their perspectives to inform inclusive curriculum design and delivery.

Even if your school doesn't adopt this particular framework, it is important that some kind of formal evaluation is initiated. To carry this out, a road map involving preparation and reflection is essential to prepare teachers and clarify goals. There also has to be transparency and a shared understanding of why such a framework is useful for guiding the school in the right direction as there may be some resistance to it. The template below allows initiatives to be broken down and made more achievable.

Aow, Hollins and Whitehead (2023, pp. 169–171) propose the following **six-stage framework** which I have adapted to include examples with regard to ELT materials:

Template for a school's initiatives

1 Current practice

Explain an area which is functioning well in your institution, e.g. the use of some locally produced ELT materials which are more inclusive than international ones available.

2 Growth area priority

Explain how this area could grow more: research into more inclusive ELT materials which could be adopted by the school.

3 Future practice

What would be the ideal outcome (with regard to materials)? 1 For learners to see themselves represented in the materials used in the school, bearing in mind its demographics and that of the local community. 2 For learners to input their own ideas for ELT materials used in the school.

4 Areas in need of strengthening

Behaviours and mindsets: Awareness of unequal representation in materials within the teaching staff.

Systems and structures: Commitment to prioritize finding inclusive materials for all ages and levels.

5 Understanding gaps and misconceptions

CPD (Continuous Professional Development) with regard to what are inclusive materials and getting teachers to analyse materials with a critical eye. Teacher training sessions to give tips on how to get students to create their own materials if there are gaps.

6 Next steps
Initiative options

Keep using the existent inclusive materials.
Phase out outdated non-inclusive materials.
Start researching new options and how to obtain them.

Timeline/Timeframe

Medium/Long term initiative: New materials to be introduced gradually so as not to overwhelm teachers.

Advocates/Allies

Identify those who can push these ideas forward within the school and in the community (e.g. local publishers, other stakeholders).

Resources commitment

Consider giving a group of senior teachers an official role in analysing and selecting new teaching materials.

Evidence of progress

The groups in charge of selecting materials should monitor progress by updating lists of potential materials and documenting their findings.

Transparency

Set communication goals to share progress in materials selection, addressing challenges and celebrating milestones. Involve parents and other stakeholders in order to gain their approval for these changes.

Aow, A., Holins, A. and Whitehead, S. (2023) *Becoming a Totally Inclusive School: A Guide for Teachers and School Leaders*. Routledge.

G: Problematizing inclusion

In this closing section, I suggest alternative ways that we can approach inclusion to make the subject and its discourse more human, less polarizing and fundamentally kinder in focus.

30   Closing thoughts

30   Closing thoughts

> The problem may well lie with the concept of *inclusion* itself and the way it can be so easily politicised and even appropriated by those who oppose an inclusive agenda.

When I embarked on this project, friends and colleagues praised the endeavour, but I did get the odd remark, such as, 'Watch out, you know you're bound to offend someone' or the more cynical, 'Are you sure being White, gay, male and Jewish makes you sufficiently qualified to write this?' These comments revealed the complexity of the topic and the extent to which my work would be scrutinized. But they also showed how strongly people feel about it and how easy it is to 'slip up' if you're not careful.

Despite these risks, I decided to press on with the project because I felt the ELT industry was falling dangerously behind with regard to inclusive practice. However, as I dug deeper into inclusion, I began to be more critical of its discourse and to appreciate why some language teachers might feel that inclusion is not for them. These insights pushed me all the more to write the book: I felt it was more important and necessary than ever. But at the same time, I knew that I could not finish it without making some critical conclusions.

This final section should therefore be read as a deeply personal reflection. It tackles the broader issues surrounding inclusion and looks at how we can critique and problematize the concept in a positive way. It is less about pedagogy and more about the world surrounding language teaching, the culture of inclusion and how that may impact our work now and in the future. It certainly does not intend to undermine inclusion, nor the 29 ideas that precede this one. It simply sets out to acknowledge the topic's complexity and the need to analyse inclusion with greater nuance and sensitivity.

Inclusive language

Inclusive language emerged from the need to examine how certain words and phrases serve to reinforce prejudiced ways of thinking and a dominant culture and exclude those on the margins. However, I believe that this notion of 'slipping up' has also emerged from these language choices. To my mind, there is a lack of self-criticism in the field and many arguments which take a high moral tone about what is right and wrong only simplify more complex scenarios. This is particularly true when it comes to analysing the correct linguistic terms to use (see **6**).

Indeed, I can't help feeling at times that we are on what the linguist Stephen Pinker (1994) termed the 'euphemism treadmill' whereby a term becomes stigmatized and has to be rapidly replaced with another more inclusive one. These new terms also confuse as sometimes they stick and sometimes they don't. For example, when this book went to press, the term *unhoused* had not yet replaced *homeless* in popular usage, but I was conscious of its existence and the reasons why it was being promoted. I thought of adopting it but then I wondered how long would it be before *unhoused* was also considered stigmatizing by some? And, more importantly, I wondered what would a person who sleeps in the streets prefer to be called? Perhaps nobody has bothered to ask them.

Often the problem lies in the eagerness to coin these new labels and to police the old ones. Many terms such as **BIPOC** or *Latinx* (see **3**) are intended to be inclusive, but they are distracting and can actually bewilder and end up alienating parts of the population. They then become easy targets for those who like to classify such terms as **virtue signaling** or 'woke'. Worse still, our well-intentioned new labels could themselves become example of linguistic colonialism. For example, the term *Latinx* may sound like the right thing to say in academic circles, but does it actually reflect the preferences of Latin Americans? Would they use it to describe themselves? Such terminology may ultimately antagonize and polarize the debate still further. As Naomi Klein (2023, p. 127) put it: 'it's not a great secret that plenty of people routinely go too far, turning minor language infractions into major crimes, while adopting a discourse that is so complex and jargon-laden that people outside university settings often find it off-putting – or straight-up absurd.' Indeed, the emphasis on how non-inclusive language manifests itself, for example, in **microaggressions** (see **11**), can also give the impression that **discrimination** and prejudice is so embedded in society that we are somehow destined not to understand each other. This sets up an 'us' versus 'them' divide, focusing on what separates us rather than on what we have in common.

Censorship and controversy

Every day in the news, there are depressing reports about one authority or another censoring teaching material of some kind. But are these situations as cut and dried as they seem? Is it only conservatives who do this kind of thing? These days, warnings of all kinds are found in other contexts where sometimes the arguments are more complex. For example, a liberal leaning newspaper such as The Guardian (4.1.24) recently criticized the policy of showing trigger warnings before the projection of James Bond movies.

Likewise, the estate of Roald Dahl recently hired a group of sensitivity readers to create more inclusive versions of his books. Some defended the changes because of the racist and sexist stereotypes present, while others protested that such changes were a form of censorship and went against Dahl's wishes. The books are a product of their time, and therefore should be read and enjoyed within their historical context. Whatever your opinion (Dahl is clearly a polarizing figure), I think it is important to remember that rewriting of this kind sets a dangerous precedent. If Roald Dahl can be rewritten, the same can be done to any text and according to any criteria. In the end, nobody 'won' this polarized debate between 'offence management' and censorship. Faced by the controversy, Dahl's publishers Penguin ultimately decided to retain both versions, rebranding the originals as 'The Classical Collection' (a euphemism if ever there was one!).

Uncomfortable truths

When problematizing inclusion, we must also reflect on our own privileges (see **5**) and the inherent contradictions involved in identifying inequities or preaching about issues of inclusion from positions of relative comfort. Researching for this book, I have read a plethora of books and articles on the above topics but the majority of these are written from the point of view of academics in comfortable positions in North American and European universities. I am not such a person, but I am certainly speaking from a position of extreme privilege. However **marginalized** I may have felt in my life due to my gay or Jewish identity, I am, of course, not in any way as 'oppressed' as most of the people I write about (see **3**).

Likewise, it is fine to talk about social justice but when we do this from the comfort of exclusive, private-sector organizations there is an undeniable disconnect. As Philip Kerr (2023, p. 21) said in the chapter on Inclusion in his *30 Trends in ELT*, we should be aware that particular sets of values can easily conflict with others. It is hard to disagree with this: 'How, for example, does my belief in the importance of equality of educational opportunity sit with the belief of many socio-economically privileged parents that they have the right to select and pay for the kinds of private education that are more likely to help their children achieve high proficiency in English?'

Beyond division: A shift in the discourse

Though my position is, of course, pro-inclusive whilst writing this book, I have realized that adopting extreme stances could actually be harming our joint endeavour. Don't get me wrong, I am not suggesting an apolitical response. As Paulo Freire (1985, p. 122) famously said, 'Washing one's hands of the conflict between the powerful and the powerless means to side with the powerful, not to be neutral.' However, if we *only* see the world in terms of 'us and them' are we in danger of creating the same kind of fixed and intransigent ideology that we want to oppose? Are we, in fact, risking the creation of a newly excluded majority?

EDI departments are well-intentioned but is what they do at times just exacerbating these existing divides? Is it leading to more resentment and defensiveness from the dominant culture? And do all inclusive arguments have to be posited in those terms? If we only frame human relations as power struggles between oppressors and oppressed, are we just unwittingly empowering those who oppose inclusive practice?

It strikes me that one of the problems in all this is precisely the term *inclusion* and the discourse that surrounds it. The way inclusion is talked about gives some people (even the liberal-minded) the impression that it is impossible to be 'totally inclusive'. There is always the fear that someone will be left out of the equation – yet another example of 'slipping up'. However, inclusive practices should not revolve around scrambling to include everybody: this is an impossible and fruitless task. It is much more about being aware of those who are frequently excluded in society and acting to redress the balance. There is a difference between the two things, but that difference is often blurred to my mind.

The other reason that terms like *inclusion* are problematic is that they can be easily appropriated by others for their own ends, such as when right-wing political agitators accuse leftists and liberals of de-humanizing, and effectively '**othering**', them. Klein (2023) makes the point that this weakens the term and makes it harder for it to be used effectively. Perhaps because of that, the University of Michigan (2024) – a flagbearer for inclusive practice since 2013 – chose to rebrand its teaching programmes, switching the label from 'inclusive' to 'equitable'.

At the start of this book, I made the point that many EDI departments have started to add *Belonging* into their title descriptions, in fact the acronym EDIB is almost as prevalent now as EDI. Perhaps this is a result of some people's opposition to or lack of affinity with the term *inclusion*, or because the term has been captured to such an extent by the 'opposition': that it has lost its meaning, as Klein suggests.

Whatever the reasons, I would argue that shifting the discourse to emphasize belonging is more than just a case of tweaking the terminology. Belonging should be our ultimate goal here, the result, in reality, of all our EDI work. On a practical level, this means building a sense of community in class – 'designing learning environments where there are multiple ways to develop relationships [and] practise caring for one another.' This can be done by allowing 'learners to share their perspectives on what belonging and community can feel like and their ideas for different ways to foster belonging and community' (CAST, 2024).

I believe that this delivers an inherently more positive, accessible message than referring to inclusion alone. Though we have unpacked the term *inclusion* a great deal in this book, the fact remains that, to many people, inclusion simply refers to the act of including someone as a part of a group, whereas belonging refers to the *feeling* of being part of a group – something we have all experienced. Inclusion may, therefore, be seen as something a dominant group bestows on others, while belonging emerges from meaningful and mutual contribution to any group. As the UDL says, belonging highlights the need to 'cultivate spaces where learners are wanted and where learners want to be' (CAST, 2024).

Conclusion: Kindness and community

In this book, I have tried not to follow the path of **differentiation** and its focus on catering for special, individual needs. The approach here has been a holistic and communal one, focusing not on what separates us but rather on what can unite us, what we can share (see **Why I wrote this book**). That is the message that I think we need to spread going forward when we speak about 'being inclusive'.

An alternative framework for effective inclusive practice could therefore be based around the idea of community which clearly has a strong affinity with the notion of belonging. Both terms, to my mind, refer to a shared environment for learning where both differences and similarities can be celebrated. Community is not about maintaining an ethos of division but about respect and collaboration, about celebrating pluralism. It recognizes that our identities are not fixed but shift, that our lives are enriched by contact with others, that getting to know the other can help us understand our place in the world. I feel that incorporating these two related ideas – community and belonging – could help us reach more people in the future, not just those already convinced by the message.

Of course, the choices we make are ideological, but I feel there is a way to discuss inclusion without increasing polarization of views. For me, inclusion and the way we talk about it should highlight curiosity, empathy and respect for the other. It's not just about noticing what is bad but building what is good. Essentially, it is about caring, sharing and showing kindness to the person we have in front of us: it is about being human and fully present. This quotation from Amia Srinivasan

(2020), from an article on the use of personal pronouns, sums up my take on this:

'We can [use non-standard pronouns] because we buy into the idea that there is no simple sex or gender binary, or because we want a world in which the binary, whether it exists or not, is stripped of its cultural weight. But we can also respect people's pronouns simply because we want to be kind … because when we talk about someone, we want them to feel that it is them we are speaking of, really and wholly.'

Bradshaw, B. (2024) *Don't blame us! Are James Bond trigger warnings really for audiences' benefit?* https://www.theguardian.com/film/2024/jan/04/james-bond-trigger-warnings-really-for-audiences-benefit

CAST (2024) Universal Design for Learning Guidelines version 3.0. Retrieved from https://udlguidelines.cast.org

Freire, P. (1985) *The Politics of Education: Culture, Power, and Liberation.* Bergin and Garvey.

Kerr, P. (2023) *30 Trends in ELT.* Cambridge University Press & Assessment.

Klein, N. (2023) *Doppelganger: A Trip into the Mirror Word.* Allen Lane.

Pinker, S. (1994) https://www.nytimes.com/1994/04/05/opinion/the-game-of-the-name.html

Srinivasan, A. (2020) He, she, one, they, ho, hus, hum, ita. *London Review of Books* Vol. 42 No. 13.

University of Michigan (2024) https://sites.lsa.umich.edu/equitable-teaching/home/about-us/

Glossary

This glossary should be referred to in combination with **1** on key concepts, **3** on reframing labels and **6** on inclusive language as certain terms are explained in greater detail there.

Please note that there is no overall consensus on which terms are preferred in inclusive practice, and that the same term may be preferred in one country or culture, by one group or individual but considered harmful or offensive elsewhere. You may have to research the context in which you are using this language carefully.

Due to space restrictions, this glossary is by no means an exhaustive list and, in particular, it does not go into great detail about inclusive language choices (e.g. using *older people* over *the elderly*) although some are offered. Likewise, it does not detail preferred culturally appropriate terms which do not refer to people, such as *informal settlements* (rather than *shanty town* or *slum*). Sadly, there are just too many of such terms to reference here.

Not all the terms mentioned here are specifically referred to in the book, but you will come across their use in reference to inclusion. Bear in mind that many terms are in flux and their connotations change, for example, some lose their harmful associations over time and others gain them. Human rights groups, advocates and stakeholders are always seeking out more inclusive alternatives to established terminology.

Finally, I have added some terms used by those opposing an inclusive agenda (e.g. *woke*), not to encourage the use of such terms but to raise awareness of how they are employed in the inclusion debate (see **30**).

Further reading

For an in-depth and historical analysis of prejudice in language, Karen Stollznow's (2020) *On the Offensive: Prejudice in Language Past and Present* is recommended, and I have quoted it on a number of occasions within the Glossary. Please also refer to the American Psychological Association's (APA) *Inclusive Language Guide* for a comprehensive list of terms. This includes examples of terms and phrases which should be avoided and suggested alternatives grouped by area of marginalization:

https://www.apa.org/about/apa/equity-diversity-inclusion/language-guidelines.

Another useful resource is the *Oxfam Inclusive Language Guide*: https://policy-practice.oxfam.org/resources/inclusive-language-guide-621487/ This includes a useful checklist (p. 14) entitled 'Questions To Ask Yourself' regarding to inclusive language use. It is worth reflecting on these five questions when considering the terms that you use in any given moment:

- *Who am I including and who am I excluding through the use of this language?*
- *Am I inadvertently ignoring or erasing individuals or groups who experience discrimination by not understanding the impacts of my language?*
- *Am I reinforcing the norms that I wish to disrupt through this language or challenging these norms and assumptions?*
- *Am I over-generalizing and making assumptions about what my audience will and won't understand?*
- *Am I making conscious choices about the language I use … or am I falling into old habits?*

ableism: discriminatory attitudes, policies, behaviours or rules that lead to unfair or harmful treatment of **disabled** people and an unfair advantage to people who are not disabled.

accommodations: to make special arrangements so that a person with different needs from others can do something they need to do: in our context these can be in the form of *presentation* (how students access information), *response* (how they present their work in different ways), *setting* or changes in the location or conditions of learning and *timing*.

ADHD (attention deficit hyperactivity disorder): a condition which can include differences in focusing and maintaining attention and having excessive energy levels. This may manifest itself in class in differences in following instructions and uncertainty in social interaction.

affirmative action: the policy of giving preference to groups who are often treated unfairly (e.g. disabled people), when choosing job candidates, accessing education or political posts.

ageism: prejudice and discriminatory attitudes levelled at people because of their age. Though it does not only refer to discrimination against older people, it is often used to describe a tendency within society to fail to respond to this age group's needs. It is one of the *-isms* that is hardest to recognize as it is embedded in so many common messages. For more information and useful advice about teaching older people, see Kieran Donaghy's blog: https://kierandonaghy.com/seven-factors-bear-mind-teaching-older-students/

ally: a person, often a member of a privileged and/or dominant group, who supports members of other marginalized groups. An ally does not show sympathy for those who experience discrimination, but advocates for them and takes action to support them.

allyship: using a position of privilege to help people from marginalized groups. This should be done without expectation of reward or thanks but to show solidarity and support. Dabiri's (2021) *What White People Can Do Next: From Allyship to Coalition* critiques the concept, suggesting that most allyship is performative and often motivated by praise or positive feedback in social media.

antisemitism: unfair treatment, hostility or hatred levelled at people because they are Jewish. It is considered important to spell antisemitism without a hyphen.

asylum seeker: a person who leaves their own country, often for political reasons or because of war, and seeks international protection in another. Such people haven't been legally recognized as refugees. Seeking asylum is a human right.

autism/ASC (Autism Spectrum Condition): neurological condition that affects the development of social and communication skills in ways that can make someone's behaviour and interests different from those without it. An autistic profile may include differences in social interaction and limited or repetitive patterns of behaviour. Autism can be thought of existing on a **spectrum,** but this should not be seen as a continuum ranging from a serious to a mild condition (or high or low-functioning) but rather as a mosaic where different characteristics co-occur and are not neatly arranged. There is a high degree of overlap in neurodivergent people, for example, a good number of people with ADHD also have autism (see **11**).

bias: the action of supporting or opposing a particular person or thing in an unfair way, as a result of allowing personal, subjective opinions or prejudices to influence your judgement (see **11**).

Black: generally referring to people of African or Afro-Caribbean origin. The term *Black* is often capitalised as a reference to a specific identity and community, including for those people who don't know their specific ethnic heritage. Especially in a US context, be aware of the distinction between Black and African-American as the two terms are not interchangeable. As Stollznow (2020, p. 19) says, the latter 'perpetuates the myth that all black American people come from Africa, or implies that they are immigrants who were born in Africa' (see **6**).

BIPOC: an American acronym standing for Black, Indigenous, People of Colour. The term emerged as an alternative to *People of Colour* to highlight that Black and Indigenous groups suffer unique experiences of racism. However, like the UK-originated term BAME (Black, Asian, Minority, Ethnic), the term has been criticized for placing people in one homogeneous group (see **6, 30**).

bold space (UK/Europe), brave space (USA/International): spaces which encourage individuals to engage in challenging conversations and confront biases and privileges outside their comfort zone. Distinct from the concept of a **safe space**, this is a place where courageous action is taken by all identity groups.

cisgender/cis: used to describe a person whose gender identity aligns with the body they were born with or their assigned sex at birth.

classism: unfair treatment or negative opinions about someone based on their social class (economic and social position in society). A set of practices which assign value to people according to their socio-economic status thus resulting in differential treatment. It is possibly the *-ism* least covered in inclusive discourse.

critical incident: significant events (either positive or negative) that can be used for reflection and thus improve practice. 'A person using the **critical incident method** must describe a behaviour in retrospect, or after the fact, rather than as the activity unfolds'. (https://dictionary. cambridge.org/dictionary/english/critical-incident-method)

cultural appropriation: taking or using things from a culture that is not your own, often without understanding or respecting that culture. Commonly used when members of a dominant culture seek to appropriate aspects of another culture or discourse for exploitative reasons (see **30**). The concept of cultural appropriation has, however, been critiqued for encouraging a monocultural vision of the world. Arguments, for example, about which foods belong to which culture could seem counterproductive in an increasingly gloablized world.

dead-naming: calling a transgender or a non-binary person by the name that they no longer use because it matched the gender they were said to have at birth. As Stollznow (2020 p. 94) says, '[*deadnaming*] is invalidating and disrespectful to transgender people and can effectively 'out' them, and expose them to discrimination and harassment.'

decolonization: resistance against the historical domination of cultural groups (e.g. Indigenous) by more powerful outsiders (colonizers) and the impact that this has had (e.g. displacement and oppression). *Decolonization* refers to the process of undoing the injustice, harm and exclusion that result from both historical and present-day colonization. The term *decolonizing the curriculum* refers to examining a curriculum's limitations and biases and any omissions it may have due to the effect of colonialism on educational policy.

differentiation: sometimes referred to as *individualization*, a method of designing and delivering content, products or the learning environment to best reach every learner (for example, in a 'mixed ability' class). It is important that learners do not feel marginalized by being treated differently and for this reason the term is not as commonly used as it was. For example, rather than give students different content according to their level, it may be better to give all students the same input but tier it with difficulty starting from a more basic level and moving to a higher one. Students can thus work through it at their own pace.

digital divide: the gap between those who can benefit from digital technology and those who cannot. In today's world, people without digital skills due to their lack of a device or an internet connection may feel socially excluded because their job and educational prospects will be diminished (see **12, 17**).

disability: a condition or difference (of a physical, mental or cognitive nature) that means someone faces barriers that non-disabled people don't. These barriers could be environmental, attitudinal or organizational. It is preferable to say *a person affected by a disability* which avoids negative connotations. For people without a disability, use the term *non-disabled* rather than *able-bodied*.

Note: Use **person-** or **identity-first language** (see **3**) as appropriate for the community or person being discussed. Identity-first language is preferred by some people in neurodivergent communities (e.g. the autistic community).

disabled: having a condition or difference (of a physical, mental or cognitive nature) that means someone faces barriers that non-disabled people do not, due to the way society is set up (see **social model**). *Disabled person* is preferred to *person with a disability* in many countries because of the social model's impact, but the latter is still in common use in the US. Avoid deficit terms that imply restriction (e.g. *challenged*, *impaired*, *bound*). Note: It is considered offensive to refer to *the disabled* as a group; refer to *disabled people* instead.

discrimination: unfair and differential treatment of people both at the individual, institutional or systemic level. This treatment favours certain groups over others, restricting opportunities for the latter. It may be invisible to those who hold a position of power and privilege in society. Passive discrimination refers to those circumstances where discrimination can develop without direct action, but due to cultural conventions, unfair social norms, etc.

displaced person: a person forced to leave their home because of persecution, war, poverty, disaster or other causes such as lack of educational or work opportunities. Often seen as a more inclusive and less stigmatizing label than *refugee*. *Forced displacement* is often used to describe the involuntary movement of people away from their homes.

disruption: an approach to writing inclusive materials. As Seburn (2021, p. 64) says, this approach highlights 'particular characteristics and experiences of marginalized individuals to help learners make connections to themselves, question things we may take for granted, and suggest improvements.' This differs from the **usualization** approach because 'we intentionally draw attention to the specific experiences of being marginalized' (see **21**).

erasure: denial of recognition and removal (e.g. from instructional materials) of those who are not considered worthy of inclusion.

ethnicity: a group of people with a shared culture, language, history, set of traditions, etc., or the fact of belonging to one of these groups. Some consider this to be a social construct (like race) that divides people into smaller social groups based on characteristics such as sense of group membership, values, behavioural patterns, political and economic interests and ancestry.

exclusion: social exclusion occurs when people cannot fully participate in or contribute to society because of the denial of civil, political, social, economic and cultural rights. Exclusion can result in associated problems such as unemployment, low income, poor health, etc.

gender: a way of grouping people, usually based on stereotypical characteristics or expectations, including behaviour, clothing and activities. Gender is an important part of many people's sense of self (their *gender identity*). A person's gender may or may not correspond to their *sex* assigned at birth. In addition, a person may be a certain gender and yet not wish to conform to all the societal expectations of how people of that gender should act or present themselves.

Note: Do not assume gender binaries when addressing or describing people; sometimes simply removing the gender reference can be enough (for example: *spouses and partners* instead of *husbands and wives*) (see **6**). However, remember that people respond differently in different contexts. For example, in some circles, the commonly used greeting, *Hi guys* is now considered gender neutral, whereas others regard it as *sexist* and avoid using it at all cost.

global majority: a term that encourages those of African, Asian, Latin American and Arab descent to recognize that together they comprise the majority (around 80 percent) of people in the world. Understanding that the White majority is not the global norm has the power to disrupt and recentre conversations on race and ethnicity. This term has substituted others such as *the developing world* as it is considered more empowering.

Global South: refers to the regions of Latin America, Asia, Africa and Oceania that are mostly low-income and often politically or culturally marginalized as opposed to the Global North which includes the economic powers of North America and Europe. The term focuses on geopolitical power relations and is often used to discuss systemic inequalities stemming from globalization and the consequences of colonialism. Though commonly found in inclusive discourse, it is an imperfect term from a geographical point of view (e.g. Australia is in the Global South) and has been criticized for creating simplistic and inaccurate polarities. However, established ways of perceiving the globe such as *Western world* or *the West* are not considered inclusive as they are too Eurocentric and too deeply rooted in colonization.

Note: Regarding geographical location, it is preferable to talk about specific places to avoid generalization or homogenization of different countries or cultures. So, instead of referring to *African* or *African culture*, refer to the particular town, city, country or culture in question. This also pertains to the use of *American*, where the latter is often used to refer to the US exclusively. Also bear in mind that other indiscriminate terms such as *Asian* can have different meanings in different countries. For example, in Australia the term often refers to people from East Asia, while in the UK it more commonly refers to people of South Asian origin.

heteronormative, heteronormativity: cultural and social practices and power structures that suggest only heterosexual relationships are normal and that men and women have naturally different roles.

Hispanic/Latino: when talking to people who identify as Hispanic or Latino, it is always best to consult with the individuals concerned. *Latino/a* is gendered but bear in in mind that non-gendered alternatives such as *Latinx* and other terms that use the *x* suffix may be more commonly used by academics and journalists than by the people they are describing (see **30**).

immigrant: a person who moves from one country to another with a view to live there and gain permanent residence. Be aware that the term is often misused to refer to naturalized residents. Also **migrant**, a person who travels to a different country or within their own country, often due to greater employment opportunities. Stollznow (2020, p. 33) says, 'even the seemingly neutral terms *immigrant* and *migrant* have acquired negative connotations, tarnished through association to words such as *alien* and *illegal*.' Likewise, avoid the use of *economic migrant* as it often implies that somebody has moved for personal convenience to earn a better living, taking the benefits of their destination's population.

Indigenous: (usually capitalized) the original people of a territory and/ or any group who are historically or ancestrally native to a specific region. However, in order to avoid homogenization, where possible name specific groups in the way they wish to be referred to (e.g. Inuit, Quechua, Māori). If speaking in general, refer to an Indigenous group as a *people* or *nation* but not as *indigenous people of the USA* as such people may not identify with the country but rather see themselves as nations in their own right. *First nations* (*people*) or *first people* are other terms that can be used. The term *aboriginal* should be avoided.

Islamophobia: discrimination, prejudice, hostility and hateful rhetoric aimed toward Islam and Muslims. Islamophobia may be based on ideas about Islam as a religion or about Muslims as a cultural and ethnic group. Given this ambiguity surrounding its use, *anti-Muslim prejudice* is often the preferred term (see Stollznow, 2020, p. 145).

Muslims may experience intersectional discrimination and stereotyping. For example, Muslim men may be stereotyped as violent and Muslim women as lacking control over their own lives. As Stollznow (2020, p. 147) says, 'This is a type of ethnocentrism … [in which] the West is rational, developed, humane, and superior, while the Middle East is portrayed as irrational, undeveloped, inhumane and inferior. In this 'us and them' mentality, Muslim people are positioned as 'the other'… [and] … cast as the enemy.'

LGBTQIA+: acronym for lesbian, gay, bisexual, transgender, queer, intersex, asexual (+ other identities): relating to or characteristic of people whose sexual orientation is not heterosexual, or whose gender identity is not cisgender. In some contexts, the Q stands for 'questioning', referring to somebody who is still exploring their sexuality or gender identity.

In North America, '2S', meaning 'two-spirit' is sometimes added, particularly where this term has historically been used in Indigenous culture. If in doubt, refer to those with specialist knowledge in your context. The acronym's complex and ever-changing status can be distracting and even off-putting to some people and you will still see other shorter forms used, such as LGBTQ or LGBT(+), though these are considered too restrictive by many (see **6**).

marginalized: to treat someone as if they were not important (on the margins). The adjective is frequently used with *identities* and *communities* to refer to those excluded from dominant social groups. Marginalization often occurs because of unequal power relationships between such groups.

medical model (of disability): views disability as a problem of the person, as a deviation from the norm, caused by disease, trauma or a health condition. Management of the disability is aimed at a 'cure', via the individual's adjustment or change in behaviour.

mental health: the condition of someone's mind and whether or not they are experiencing mental health challenges or illnesses. Avoid outdated terms such *mental illness* and *mentally ill* which are now regarded as offensive. Consider using *(person with) a mental health condition* and, where possible, refer to the specific disorders such as OCD (obsessive-compulsive disorder) or bipolar disorder.

Note: Be aware that such disorders can be used as a common form of hyperbole when used to talk about everyday behaviour. 'The neighbor whose house is neat and tidy is *OCD*, while someone who is worried or self-conscious is *paranoid* … mood swings are described as *bipolar*' (Stollznow, p. 162). Such conversational misuse undermines the seriousness of such conditions, painting them as character flaws.

microaggression: statement, action or incident which can be regarded as a form of discrimination against a marginalized group on a subtle or indirect level. The prefix 'micro' has been critiqued for minimizing the importance of such statements or actions, however 'micro' here does not refer to 'small' but rather that these incidents occur often and on a micro or person-to-person level. Stollznow (2020, p. 38) goes on to say that, 'microaggressions often reveal **unconscious bias**. They are not usually intended to be discriminatory or rude, so some people are unaware of exactly why they are considered to be offensive' (see **11**).

minority: a term used to describe non-dominant social, religious, ethnic or cultural groups. Avoid using *minority* if you are addressing a specific community because it can imply an inferior social position.

neurodiverse: having a brain that functions in a way that is considered different from the 'norm' or what is usual, for example, that of a person with autism. It is important not to see neurodiverse students in terms of their difficulties but to recognize their skills. For example, many dyslexic people are highly empathic, intuitive and good at visual thinking.

neurotypical: having a brain that functions in a way that is considered the 'norm', though the meaning of the term may vary with regard to setting, location or context. It has been estimated that around 15 percent of the population have a range of neurodivergent traits that may differ from society's views of those who are considered to be neurotypical. There is not always a hard and fast line between the two.

neurodiversity: used to encompass people with **ADHD** (attention deficit hyperactivity disorder), **dyslexia, dyspraxia, dyscalculia** and other neurological differences. The umbrella term of neurodiversity is often preferred these days because it emphasizes that all brains function differently and that neuro-differences such as **autism** and **dyslexia** often co-occur. The separate labels, on the other hand, may emphasize a differentiation which may not always be desirable, hence they are not referred to in isolation in this book.

non-binary: having a gender identity that is not simply male or female: *gender neutral* or *gender fluid* can also be used. *Non-binary* refers to people who don't identify as either male or female but are on various places on the gender spectrum. You may also hear people describe themselves as 'Enby': currently a slang term for non-binary (*NB* is the abbreviation).

norm: a perceived, accepted or standard way of behaving or doing things. Often combined with *social* or *societal* to refer to collective beliefs about typical behaviour which can be enforced by social sanctions or rewards, for example, *the unfair social norm* that women earn less for the same work than their male colleagues in most societies.

normative gaze: a perspective from which the world is often presented to us – White, male, middle-class, non-disabled, etc.

othering: treating a person or group as different (and often inferior) because they don't fit into a dominant culture. Othering creates an 'us versus them' dynamic, where a dominant group claims normative status and everyone outside of that group is defined in relation to it. It is also described as what happens when a group is treated as an object by another which allows the dominant group to justify its exploitation (see **22**).

People of Colour: collective term for people who are racialized as other than White. The term is frequently used but is problematic in that it defines people in relation to Whiteness and treats them as a homongenous 'non-White' group. (see **BIPOC**) (see **6, 30**). On the other hand, Stollznow (2020, p. 19) says, 'It may be *people of colour* is acceptable because it uses person-first language, highlighting their humanity over skin colour.'

positionality: a person's social position in relation to age, gender, language, sexual orientation, socioeconomic status, etc. bearing in mind systems of privilege and oppression. 'Positionality statements' are quite common in the educational context, in particular in research (see **5**). For example, if a researcher makes such a statement about their identity at the beginning of their work, it can give useful insights into their general outlook and how they approach a topic.

queer: originally used in a derogatory way to describe LGBTQIA+ people, it has now been reclaimed to refer to different sexual orientations and/or gender identities that do not fit society's **heteronormativity.** It tends to be used positively by queer people themselves, but it remains an offensive label for some (see **6**).

race: constructed social groups into which humans are divided artificially according to perceived similarities in their physical characteristics (as opposed to cultural ones). Now an outdated historical concept, *race* is no longer recognized as a biologically valid classification. Our genetic differences should not define our character, abilities or identity. Avoid the term *mixed race*; it is better to say *dual heritage*, *bi-racial* or *multi-racial*.

racialize: to categorize according to 'race'. This can relate to an identity, a group of people, society or a problem. When referring to a collective noun, it may be preferable to use *racialized community* rather than an acronym such as *BIPOC*.

racism: policies, rules, behaviours, etc. that result in a continued unfair advantage given to some people and unfair or harmful treatment given to others; harmful or unfair things that people say, do, or think based on the belief that their own perceived 'race' makes them superior to people of other perceived 'races'. *Racism* can be used to refer not only to intentional or unintentional actions by an individual but to systems that perpetuate inequality on a broader scale. We can speak of *institutionalized racism*, *structural racism* and *systemic racism* to describe such policies, practices and laws in which discrimination is embedded in society and how it operates.

refugee: a person who has left their country because of persecution and serious human rights violations. Their own government cannot or will not protect them from those dangers. Refugees have a right to international protection. Stollznow (2020, p. 32) says that, 'Stakeholders tend to eschew refugee as a self-identifying label, because it is perceived as dehumanizing and distancing and carries with it the stigma and trauma of their experiences.'

Roma: (also *Romani*) an ethnic group of traditionally itinerant people who originated in northern India but now live worldwide, mostly in Europe. They have long experienced discrimination from society. Using the word *gypsy* is considered a racist term in some contexts, however, it is still used by some Roma organizations in others.

safe space: a place or a situation where you feel protected from harm or danger. It also can be used to describe a theoretical or cognitive space, not necessarily a physical one.

SEN(D): an acronym for *special educational needs (and disability)*. It refers to students with physical or neurodiverse differences and/ or disabilities and is often locally defined as an aspect of educational policy. It is still the preferred term in many contexts but is starting to lose favour in educational ones, such as ELT. In particular, you should avoid saying *person with SEN*. Depending on the difference in question, it is preferable to say *disabled person* or *neurodiverse person* (see **3**).

sexism: Stollznow (2020, pp. 55–56) defines sexism as, 'attitudes, beliefs and behaviours that reflect negative evaluations on the basis of sex and gender … (It) can involve the unequal treatment of people based on their sex, and includes institutional and cultural practices that treat people unfairly, such as the gender gap in hiring and the gender pay gap. … It includes the objectification of people in the media and advertising … and sexist language… that abuses, belittles, or undervalues … Sexism can affect anyone, but it primarily affects women and girls … According to the way we talk, men are usually represented as the default sex, while women are talked about as subordinate, secondary … or 'the other'.'

sizeism: bias against people because of their body size. Like other forms of bias and discrimination, sizeism can have a negative effect on an individual's physical health and well-being. Try to avoid making unsolicited comments about body sizes or changes and using terms such as *ideal/preferred weight*.

social model (**of disability**): in this model, people are 'disabled' by barriers operating in society that are excluding and discriminating. Here, disability is not a characteristic of an individual, but a social construct, while it is the environment that fails to appropriately accommodate the needs of people with disabilities. From this perspective, equal access to resources for someone with a disability is a human rights issue (see **2**).

tokenism: something that a person or organization does that seems to support or help people who are treated unfairly in society, but which is not meant to make changes that would help in a lasting way. Such actions may only serve to prevent criticism, give the impression of diversity, or tick boxes (see **18**).

transgender: (also **trans**) used to describe a person whose gender identity is not the same as the one they were assigned at birth. Do not use *transgender* as a noun, and avoid the word *transsexual* (whether as an adjective or noun) unless the person you are talking about has made it clear that this is the term they prefer (see **23**).

universal design: design of products, environments and services to be usable by all students to the greatest extent possible, with no need for specialized adaptations. The UDL guidelines were created by CAST: https://udlguidelines.cast.org

usualization: an approach to writing inclusive materials. The term in this context was originally coined by Sanders in opposition to the term *normalization*: http://the-classroom.org.uk/how-to-do-it/usualising-and-actualising/method-1-usualising/

As Seburn (2021, p. 60) says, this form of representation of marginalized groups does not highlight 'the 'specialness' (or 'strangeness' rather) of individuals … [and aims] to spread their narratives alongside all others with regular frequency. [In this way] … we increase exposure to a variety of members from these groups and a variety of voices. Here, we aim for everyone's identity to be 'usual' within a society' (see **21**).

virtue signalling: an attempt to show to others that you are a good person, for example, by expressing opinions that will be acceptable to them, often on social media. The term is often used to describe people whose actions or opinions may be virtuous in a superficial way and/or merely demonstrate a high moral tone.

White: a person who considers themselves to be White or is racialized as White. People of various ethnic groups may be racialized as White or non-white even if they do not identity as such. Stollznow (2020, p.18) says that the '*white/non-white* binary is problematic because it presents white people as colourless, the norm, first, superior, and as some kind of standard against which all other kinds of people are compared' (see **6**).

White gaze: assumes that the person reading or viewing something is White and regards White culture as the default experience. Assuming our audiences are White means we cater only for these views and overlook other experiences, norms and cultures.

Whiteness: ideology that privileges White people over non-White people in a hierarchical society (see **6**).

White privilege: benefits and advantages held by White people in society solely because they are White. People may be unconscious of these privileges because they have become institutionalized.

woke: aware of social problems such as racism and injustice. Originally having positive connotations, it is now often used in a pejorative way, especially by those attacking an inclusive agenda.

Index